A BASIC GUIDE TO

Skiing and Snowboarding

An Official U.S. Olympic Committee Sports Series

The U.S. Olympic Committee

Griffin Publishing Group

This Hardcover Edition Distributed By
Gareth Stevens Publishing
A World Almanac Education Group Company

This hardcover edition distributed by
Gareth Stevens Publishing
A World Almanac Education Group Company
330 West Olive Street, Suite 100
Milwaukee, WI 53212 USA
Please visit our web site at: www.garethstevens.com

For a free color catalog describing Gareth Stevens' list of high-quality books and multimedia programs, call 1-800-542-2595 or fax your request to (414) 332-3567.

Library of Congress Cataloging-in-Publication Data for this hardcover edition available upon request from Gareth Stevens Publishing. Fax (414) 336-0157 for the attention of the Publishing Records Department.

Hardcover edition: ISBN 0-8368-3104-7

Editorial Statement
In the interest of brevity, the Editors have chosen to use the standard English form of address. Please be advised that this usage is not meant to suggest a restriction to, nor an endorsement of, any individual or group of individuals, either by age, gender, or athletic ability. The Editors certainly acknowledge that boys and girls, men and women, of every age and physical condition are actively involved in sports, and we encourage everyone to enjoy the sports of his or her choice.

1 2 3 4 5 6 7 8 9 06 05 04 03 02
Printed in the United States of America

ACKNOWLEDGMENTS

PUBLISHER   Griffin Publishing Group
DIR. / OPERATIONS   Robin L. Howland
PROJECT MANAGER   Bryan K. Howland
WRITER   Mark Maier
BOOK DESIGN   m2design group

USOC
CHAIRMAN/PRESIDENT   Sandra (Sandy) Baldwin

U.S. SKI AND SNOWBOARD ASSOCIATION
CHAIRMAN   Jim McMarthy
PRESIDENT AND CEO   Bill Marolt
EDITOR   Geoffrey M. Horn

PHOTOS   ALLSPORT
COVER DESIGN   m2design group
COVER PHOTO   Steve Powell/ALLSPORT
ATHLETE ON COVER   Picabo Street

THE UNITED STATES OLYMPIC COMMITTEE

The U.S. Olympic Committee (USOC) is the custodian of the U.S. Olympic Movement and is dedicated to providing opportunities for American athletes of all ages.

The USOC, a streamlined organization of member organizations, is the moving force for support of sports in the United States that are on the program of the Olympic and/or Pan American Games, or those wishing to be included.

The USOC has been recognized by the International Olympic Committee since 1894 as the sole agency in the United States whose mission involves training, entering, and underwriting the full expenses for the United States teams in the Olympic and Pan American Games. The USOC also supports the bid of U.S. cities to host the winter and summer Olympic Games, or the winter and summer Pan American Games, and after reviewing all the candidates, votes on and may endorse one city per event as the U.S. bid city. The USOC also approves the U.S. trial sites for the Olympic and Pan American Games team selections.

Welcome to the Olympic Sports Series

We feel this unique series will encourage parents, athletes of all ages, and novices who are thinking about a sport for the first time to get involved with the challenging and rewarding world of Olympic sports.

This series of Olympic sport books covers both summer and winter sports, features Olympic history and basic sports fundamentals, and encourages family involvement. Each book includes information on how to get started in a particular sport, including equipment and clothing; rules of the game; health and fitness; basic first aid; and guidelines for spectators. Of special interest is the information on opportunities for senior citizens, volunteers, and physically challenged athletes. In addition, each book is enhanced by photographs and illustrations and a complete, easy-to-understand glossary.

Because this family-oriented series neither assumes nor requires prior knowledge of a particular sport, it can be enjoyed by all age groups. Regardless of anyone's level of sports knowledge, playing experience, or athletic ability, this official U.S. Olympic Committee Sports Series will encourage understanding and participation in sports and fitness.

The purchase of these books will assist the U.S. Olympic Team. This series supports the Olympic mission and serves importantly to enhance participation in the Olympic and Pan American Games.

United States Olympic Committee

Contents

U S A

AN ATHLETE'S CREED

The most important thing in the Olympic Games is not to win but to take part, just as the most important thing in life is not the triumph but the struggle. The essential thing is not to have conquered but to have fought well.

These famous words, commonly referred to as the Olympic Creed, were once spoken by Baron Pierre de Coubertin, founder of the modern Olympic Games. Whatever their origins, they aptly describe the theme behind each and every Olympic competition.

Metric Equivalents

Wherever possible, measurements given are those specified by the Olympic rules. Other measurements are given in metric or standard U.S. units, as appropriate. For purposes of comparison, the following rough equivalents may be used.

1 kilometer (km)	= 0.62 mile (mi)	1 mi = 1.61 km
1 meter (m)	= 3.28 feet (ft)	1 ft = 0.305 m
	= 1.09 yards (yd)	1 yd = 0.91 m
1 centimeter (cm)	= 0.39 inch (in)	1 in = 2.54 cm
	= 0.1 hand	1 hand (4 in) = 10.2 cm
1 kilogram (kg)	= 2.2 pounds (lb)	1 lb = 0.45 kg
1 milliliter (ml)	= 0.03 fluid ounce (fl oz)	1 fl oz = 29.573 ml
1 liter	= 0.26 gallons (gal)	1 gal = 3.785 liters

1

Skiing and the Olympics

Ask any skiing or snowboarding fans and they will tell you that nothing quite compares with the feel of fresh snow beneath their feet, the adrenaline rush of speeding downhill, and the exhilaration of a completed run. The sport has come a long way from its humble beginnings.

A Short History of Skiing

Evidence shows that humans have been skiing from before the dawn of history, mostly in the northern parts of Europe and Asia. The oldest known ski—found in a peat bog at Umea, Sweden—goes back some 45 centuries to about 2500 B.C. (when Egypt was building its pyramids). A Stone Age petroglyph showing a skier in Rodoy, Norway, has been dated at 5000 B.C., a sign that someone was on skis more than 7,000 years ago.

The word "ski" has a northern European linguistic root describing a splinter actually cut from a log. It later became the Scandinavian word for "shoe" and was pronounced "shee." A desire to improve the efficiency of land travel, especially in the ice and snow, led to the emergence of skiing, and perfection of the activity didn't take very long. Greek historians wrote about skiing, and the Chinese noted the practice in the seventh century B.C.

Through the ages, skis continued to be a staple for travel in the coldest areas of the world. Norwegian soldiers were on skis as early as 960 A.D., and Sweden had its own ski-borne troops a couple of centuries later. Skiing was a means of transportation in the Scandinavian nations of Norway, Sweden, Finland, and Denmark, four countries with rugged terrain and long, snowy winters. Since villages were far apart, most people used skis for transportation, commerce, and survival. Later, as Scandinavians emigrated to the United States, they brought their ski skills and heritage with them.

Stories are told from generation to generation about Norwegians who wore "planks" to hunt, fish, and trap game. Pine and spruce wood were used, and the devices were strapped on with leather strips made from animal hides. A shorter kicking ski was worn on the right foot, with a longer running ski on the left, which allowed the skier to move faster over snow. Early skiers also used long, sturdy, pointed sticks for poles. Even these experienced hunters and travelers were not immune to losing a ski here and there.

A famous story from Norway's history tells of the rescue of two-year-old Prince Hakon Hakonsson from kidnappers in 1296 at Lillehammer. His rescuers, outfitted with skis, carried him on their backs over a mountain range to Rena in Osterdal. More than 700 years later, their heroic effort is commemorated annually by a 55-km ski race from Lillehammer to Rena. Each skier wears a 3.5-kg backpack as a reminder of the kidnapped Prince Hakon.

By the mid-1800s, Norwegians had attached sturdy bindings to their skis, which gave them better control and made jumping and turning possible. The Norwegians skied from Norway across Sweden and Finland into Siberia, all the way to the Pacific Coast. They were the first to make Arctic expeditions on skis, and the first to use skis for delivering the mail between settlements. Eventually, skiing competitions between individuals, groups, and entire villages became popular winter sporting events.

The Rise of Modern Skiing

Military competitions that included firing rifles (the forerunner of biathlon) were held in Oslo, Norway, as early as 1767. Soldiers also competed against each other by skiing down a steep slope without leaning on their "poles" and descending a moderately steep slope between bushes without falling over, a possible precursor of the modern slalom.

The first documented ski jump took place at Huseby Hill, near Christiana, in 1879, but the real start of skiing as an actual sport dates from the 1850s, when the first downhill race was held in Oslo, Norway. Ski jumping was later added, and the competition included a trophy from the Norwegian royal family for the winner.

In those early days, skiing primarily referred to the Nordic events (ski jumping and cross-country), as there was limited downhill skiing. This changed after the British, who were the mountain climbers of Europe, reached the summit of Mt. Matterhorn at 14,691 feet (4,478 meters) in the Swiss Alps in 1865. When mountaineers began skiing down steep slopes in the Alps, alpine skiing was born. By the early 1900s, the British had founded the Public Schools Alpine Sports Club. The first English-language book about skiing, *Ski-Running*, was published in 1904.

Sondre Norheim, of Telemark County in southern Norway, is the father of modern-day skiing. In the 1870s and 1880s he used stiff bindings to hold his skis to his boots and amazed people with his ability to twist and jump and not lose his skis. Norheim won Norway's first national cross-country ski race in 1867. He also designed the Telemark ski, the model for today's skis. Telemark County skiers perfected the Telemark and Christiana (shortened now to "Christie") turns used to control speed while going downhill.

Across the Atlantic, Norwegian immigrants introduced skis to the United States early in the 19th century, although the idea of moving across and on top of snow was known to Native American peoples (as evidenced by archaeological finds). Skiing moved west to the Rocky Mountains and then to California and the Pacific Northwest as the United States was settled.

At the time of California's Gold Rush in 1849, Scandinavian miners, who brought skis or snowshoes with them from the old country, were skiing down the Sierra Nevada Mountains in what may have been the first organized ski races in America. They used 12-foot-long skis—and a secret formula wax they called "dope"—to ski faster and farther than their competitors, in their attempt to claim the $100 top prize. In a tiny town called Alturas, in the Sierra foothills, the first ski club in the U.S. was founded. This was the Alturas Snowshoe Club, which sponsored annual tournaments and cash prizes. In 1867, residents of LaPorte, Calif., organized a winter sports association with prizes up to $500 for some races.

One immigrant who made good use of skis was Jon Torsteinson Rui (whose name was Americanized to "Snowshoe Thomson") from Telemark County, Norway. Thomson was the first famous

David Cannon/ALLSPORT

Bill Koch of Team USA skis cross-country during the
1984 Winter Olympics in Sarajevo, Yugoslavia.

American cross-country skier. During the Gold Rush years, he skied the Sierra Nevada Mountains all winter to deliver the mail along a 91-mile route between Placerville, California, and Carson City, Nevada. His skis weighed 25 pounds, his pack weighed almost 100 pounds, and the one-way trip took three days, uphill. The return was shorter, only two days. Thomson made this trek for 20 years, kept to his schedule, and didn't miss a trip during his decades delivering the U.S. mail. For this, he earned $200 a month and became a U.S. Postal Service legend. Today he is remembered with a cross-country race that takes place along his old mail route.

In the 20th century, competitive skiing became the billboard for the sport, followed closely by recreational skiing. The first official national championship was held Feb. 22, 1904, in Ishpeming, Michigan, where the National Ski Association was formed a year later.

Skiing in the northeastern United States got a big boost from the activities of Fred Harris, a bored, restless student at Dartmouth College in the winter of 1909. He wanted to get students out in the fresh air and away from their card games and books, so he organized a ski club: the Dartmouth Outing Club. The club's success, which was overwhelming, led to contests between individuals on campus, annual ice carnivals, and intercollegiate competitions. The club organized what many consider the first real downhill race in the United States, at Mt. Moosilauke, New Hampshire, in April 1927. Six years later, the first U.S. national downhill championships were held. Dartmouth's skiers dominated alpine skiing through 1936, capturing more than 21 championships or trophies. They were leaders in developing skiing as both a recreational and a competitive sport.

Other factors boosted the popularity of skiing, especially after 1945. With more leisure time, more automobiles, and better highways, regular trips to ski areas became possible for larger numbers of people. The introduction of the simple rope tow, followed by chairlifts and gondolas, allowed skiers to ride up the slopes and increase the number of times they could ski down in one day. Television coverage of the Olympic Winter Games boosted not only the audience for skiing, but also the number of active participants in the sport.

Hulton Deutsch/ALLSPORT

Gretchen Fraser of Team USA wins the women's special slalom at the 1948 Winter Olympics in St. Moritz, Switzerland.

Skiing in the Olympic Games

Norwegians have had a lasting impact on the development of skiing as part of the Olympic Winter Games. As college students in Europe, many took their skis with them on holidays to Chamonix in the French Alps and skied down the mountain. They weren't afraid to jump, and with enough snow, they would use any roofs available, even that of an old barn or outbuilding, for a ski jump.

The first international governing body for skiing was the Norwegian Ski Federation, organized in Oslo, Norway, in 1910. The group continued to hold meetings and remain active on the skiing scene until World War I. The NSF was then reorganized in 1924 as the Fédération Internationale de Ski (FIS), the world governing body for skiing, during the first Olympic Winter Games, in Chamonix.

Not surprisingly, at the Chamonix Games, Norway's skiers won gold, silver, and bronze in the 50-km cross-country competition. A military patrol race, ski jumping, and an 18-km race were the other events. From then on, Norwegian skiers won more Olympic medals than skiers from any other country, except those from the former Soviet Union.

Alpine, or downhill, skiing was popular as a sport, but it would not become an Olympic event for another 12 years. A 1924 ruling by the FIS allowed only Nordic or Telemarking at the Games and World Championships.

Hosting its first Olympic Winter Games at Lake Placid, New York, in 1932, the United States saw interest in skiing soar. Resorts and ski schools opened rapidly, but the main attraction was alpine skiing. In 1936, Great Britain's efforts to include alpine skiing in the Winter Games paid off when the sport became an official event in the Olympics at Garmisch-Partenkirchen, Germany. The combined alpine event blended the results from the downhill and the slalom.

In the first three Olympic Winter Games—in 1924, 1928, and 1932—the ski events were for men only. Women participated in the inaugural alpine events in 1936, but did not compete in cross-country events until 1952. There were women on that first U.S. alpine Olympic squad, and women's races were included in the alpine national championships from the start.

Hulton Deutsch/ALLSPORT

1952 Olympic slalom champion
Andrea Mead Lawrence

For decades, Europeans continued to dominate international competition. In 1956, at Cortina d'Ampezzo, Italy, Austrian Toni Sailer became the first three-time gold medalist in alpine events. France's Jean Claude Killy

IOC Olympic Museum/ALLSPORT

Jean Claude Killy of France
en route to his triple gold-medal
performance at the 1968
Olympic Winter Games

secured another rare "triple" in alpine skiing, winning the downhill, giant slalom, and slalom events at Grenoble, France, in 1968. That feat was not achieved again until Italian Alberto Tomba won two gold medals at Calgary (1988) and his third at Albertville, France, in 1992. Another European who left his mark on the Games was Austrian Franz Klammer, who won the downhill in 1976 with speeds clocked at 80 miles per hour.

The first American to win a gold medal in skiing was Gretchen Fraser at the 1948 Games in St. Moritz, Switzerland, when she took first place in the slalom event. Giant slalom made its debut at the 1952 Winter Games in Oslo, and a 19-year-old American, Andrea Mead Lawrence, won two gold medals, in the slalom and giant slalom. Alpine skier Penny Pitou kept U.S. skiers in the medal column with two silvers in the downhill and slalom at Squaw Valley, California, in 1960. She missed the gold by one second in the downhill and 0.1 second in the giant slalom. Time favored the Americans at Sapporo, Japan, in 1972, when Barbara Ann Cochran of Team USA won the slalom event by 0.02 seconds.

Four years later, at Innsbruck, Austria, Bill Koch became the first American to medal in a Nordic event when he finished second in the 30-km race. Koch suffered from asthma, yet missed the gold by only 29 seconds.

Steve Powell/ALLSPORT

Two U.S. gold medalists show their winning form at the
1984 Olympic Winter Games in Sarajevo. Bill Johnson (above)
captured the men's downhill competition,
while Phil Mahre (below) took the men's slalom title.

ALLSPORT

Mike Powell/ALLSPORT

Olympic downhill champion Tommy Moe of Team USA practices before competing at the 1994 Winter Games in Lillehammer, Norway.

The U.S. alpine ski team brought home gold and silver medals from the Games in Sarajevo, Yugoslavia, in 1984 when Bill Johnson won the downhill and twin brothers Phil and Steve Mahre placed first and second in the slalom. At the 1992 Games in Albertville, American women captured five gold medals. Freestyle skier Donna Weinbrecht won the first Olympic women's moguls event and joined Bonnie Blair (two golds in long-track speed skating), Kristi Yamaguchi (a gold in figure skating), and Cathy Turner (a gold in short-track speed skating) as U.S. Olympic champions that year.

The 1994 Olympic Winter Games in Lillehammer, Norway, attracted 1,884 athletes from 67 countries, including 11 from the former Soviet Union. U.S. alpine skiers did well in 1994, capturing four medals. Tommy Moe took the gold in the downhill and followed that triumph a few days later, on his 24th birthday, with the silver in the men's super giant slalom. Diann Roffe-Steinrotter won the gold in the women's Super G event. Freestyle skier Liz McIntyre captured the silver medal in the women's moguls for Team USA.

At the 1998 Games in Nagano, Japan, another American, Picabo Street, took the gold in the women's Super G, while her freestyle teammates Eric Bergoust (men's aerials), Nikki Stone (women's aerials), and Jonny Moseley (men's moguls) were crowned Olympic champions in their respective specialties. Snowboarding made its debut on the Olympic program, and Americans Ross Powers and Shannon Dunn each earned a bronze medal in the men's and women's halfpipe competitions. Surprisingly, the U.S. snowboarders were shut out in the giant slalom events.

Mike Powell/ALLSPORT

Picabo Street of Team USA poses with her Olympic gold medal from the women's Super G during the 1998 Winter Games in Nagano, Japan.

Mike Powell/ALLSPORT

These two ski jump hills in Hakuba, Japan, provided a picturesque
site for the 1998 Games at Nagano.

1998 Olympic Medalists
Olympic Winter Games, Nagano, Japan

ALPINE

Men's Downhill

Gold	Jean-Luc Cretier	France
Silver	Lasse Kjus	Norway
Bronze	Hannes Trinkl	Austria

Men's Slalom

Gold	Hans-Petter Buraas	Norway
Silver	Ole Christian Furuseth	Norway
Bronze	Thomas Sykora	Austria

Men's Giant Slalom

Gold	Hermann Maier	Austria
Silver	Stefan Eberharter	Austria
Bronze	Michael Von Gruenigen	Switzerland

Men's Super Giant Slalom

Gold	Hermann Maier	Austria
Silver (tie)	Didier Cuche	Switzerland
Silver (tie)	Hans Knauss	Austria

Men's Combined

Gold	Mario Reiter	Austria
Silver	Lasse Kjus	Norway
Bronze	Christian Mayer	Austria

Women's Downhill

Gold	Katja Seizinger	Germany
Silver	Pernilla Wiberg	Sweden
Bronze	Florence Masnada	France

Women's Slalom

Gold	Hilde Gerg	Germany
Silver	Deborah Compagnoni	Italy
Bronze	Zali Steggall	Australia

Women's Giant Slalom

Gold	Deborah Compagnoni	Italy
Silver	Alexandra Meissnitzer	Austria
Bronze	Katja Seizinger	Germany

Women's Super Giant Slalom

Gold	Picabo Street	United States
Silver	Michaela Dorfmeister	Austria
Bronze	Alexandra Meissnitzer	Austria

Women's Combined

Gold	Katja Seizinger	Germany
Silver	Martina Ertl	Germany
Bronze	Hilde Gerg	Germany

CROSS-COUNTRY

Men's 10-km Classical

Gold	Bjoern Daehlie	Norway
Silver	Markus Gandler	Austria
Bronze	Mika Myllylae	Finland

Men's 15-km Freestyle/Pursuit

Gold	Thomas Alsgaard	Norway
Silver	Bjoern Daehlie	Norway
Bronze	Vladimir Smirnov	Kazakhstan

Men's 30-km Classical

Gold	Mika Myllylae	Finland
Silver	Erling Jevne	Norway
Bronze	Silvio Fauner	Italy

Men's 50-km Freestyle

Gold	Bjoern Daehlie	Norway
Silver	Niklas Jonsson	Sweden
Bronze	Christian Hoffmann	Austria

Men's 4x10-km Relay

Gold	Norway (Sture Siversten, Erling Jevne, Bjoern Daehlie, Thomas Alsgaard)
Silver	Italy (Marco Albarello, Fulvio Valbusa, Fabio Maj, Silvio Fauner)
Bronze	Finland (Harri Kirvesniem, Mika Myllylae, Sami Repo, Jari Isometsae)

Women's 5-km Classical

Gold	Larissa Lazutina	Russia
Silver	Katerina Neumannova	Czech Republic
Bronze	Benter Martinsen	Norway

Women's 15-km Classical

Gold	Olga Danilova	Russia
Silver	Larissa Lazutina	Russia
Bronze	Anita Moen-Guidon	Norway

Women's 10-km Freestyle

Gold	Larissa Lazutina	Russia
Silver	Olga Danilova	Russia
Bronze	Katerina Neumannova	Czech Republic

Women's 30-km Freestyle

Gold	Julija Tchepalova	Russia
Silver	Stefania Belmondo	Italy
Bronze	Larissa Lazutina	Russia

Women's 4x5-km Relay

Gold	Russia
Silver	Norway
Bronze	Italy

FREESTYLE

Men's Aerials

Gold	Eric Bergoust	United States
Silver	Sebastien Foucras	France
Bronze	Dmitri Dashchinsky	Belarus

Men's Moguls

Gold	Jonny Moseley	United States
Silver	Janne Lahtela	Finland
Bronze	Sami Mustonen	Finland

Women's Aerials

Gold	Nikki Stone	United States
Silver	Nannan Xu	China
Bronze	Colette Brand	Switzerland

Women's Moguls

Gold	Tae Satoya	Japan
Silver	Tatjana Mittermayer	Germany
Bronze	Kari Traa	Norway

NORDIC COMBINED

Men's Individual

Gold	Bjarte Engen Vik	Norway
Silver	Samppa Lajunen	Finland
Bronze	Valerij Stoljarov	Russia

Men's Team

Gold	Norway (Halldor Skard, Kenneth Braaten, Bjarte Engen Vik, Fred Lundberg)
Silver	Finland (Samppa Lajunen, Jari Mantila, Tapio Nurmela, Hannu Manninen)
Bronze	France (Sylvain Guillaume, Nicolas Bal, Ludovic Roux, Fabrice Guy)

SKI JUMPING

Men's 90-meter Hill

Gold	Jani Soininen	Finland
Silver	Kazuyoshi Funaki	Japan
Bronze	Andreas Widhoelzl	Austria

Men's 120-meter Hill

Gold	Kazuyoshi Funaki	Japan
Silver	Jani Soininen	Finland
Bronze	Masahiko Harada	Japan

Men's Team (120-meter Hill)

Gold	Japan (Takanobu Okabe, Hiroya Saito, Masahiko Harada, Kazuyoshi Funaki)
Silver	Germany (Sven Hannawalk, Martin Schmitt, Hansjoerg Jaekle, Dieter Thoma)
Bronze	Austria (Reinhard Schwarzenberger, Martin Hoellwarth, Stefan Horngacher, Andreas Widhoelzl)

SNOWBOARD

Men's Halfpipe

Gold	Gian Simmen	Switzerland
Silver	Daniel Franck	Norway
Bronze	Ross Powers	United States

Men's Giant Slalom

Gold	Ross Rebagliati	Canada
Silver	Thomas Prugger	Italy
Bronze	Ueli Kestenholz	Switzerland

Women's Halfpipe

Gold	Nicola Thost	Germany
Silver	Stine Brun Kjeldaas	Norway
Bronze	Shannon Dunn	United States

Women's Giant Slalom

Gold	Karine Ruby	France
Silver	Heidi Renoth	Germany
Bronze	Brigitte Koeck	Austria

2

U.S. Stars of Today

The following short biographies portray the majority of elite skiers and snowboarders on the 2001–02 U.S. ski and snowboard teams, representing U.S. medal hopes in such major events as the World Cups, National Championships, and 2002 Olympic Winter Games. Watch for these athletes as they strive for excellence on ski slopes throughout the world.

Craig Jones/ALLSPORT

Top U.S. skiers and snowboarders prepared to face the world's best at the 2002 Olympic Winter Games in Utah.

ALPINE (Men)

CHAD FLEISCHER

Height, Weight: 6' 2 1/2", 220 lb
Birthdate, Place: Jan. 4, 1972, Columbus, Neb.
Hometown: Vail, Colo.
Year on U.S. Team: 9th
School: Fort Lewis College
Club: Steamboat Springs WSC
Events: Downhill, Super G

Highlights: Two-time Olympian ('94, '98) in SG ... has 24 World Cup top-10 finishes, including 2nd in '99 World Cup finals DH and 5th in '01 season-opening DH ... 6th in '99 World Championships SG in Vail ... '96 and '99 DH national champ, '99 SG silver medalist ... began skiing at 10 on a family vacation to Colorado.

BODE MILLER

Height, Weight: 6' 2", 210 lb
Birthdate, Place: Oct. 12, 1977, Easton, N.H.
Hometown: Franconia, N.H.
Year on U.S. Team: 6th
School: Carrabassett Valley Academy
Club: CVA/Franconia
Events: Slalom, Giant Slalom, Super G

Highlights: '98 Olympian (GS, SL) ... four '01 World Cup GS top-10 finishes ... returning from a torn ACL in his left knee, suffered at the '01 World Championships, but has worked hard in rehab to come back ... '98 GS national champ ... started skiing at 3 at Cannon Mountain in New Hampshire and decided in his early teens to become a ski racer.

DARON RAHLVES

Height, Weight: 5' 9", 180 lb
Birthdate, Place: June 12, 1973, Walnut Creek, Calif.
Hometown: Sugar Bowl, Calif.
Year on U.S. Team: 9th
School: Nevada (Reno)
Events: Downhill, Giant Slalom, Super G

Highlights: '98 Olympian in SG (7th) and GS ... '01 world champ in SG ... '01 bronze medalist in Kitzbuehel's Hahnenkamm DH ... had two World Cup DH wins in 24 hours in '00 ... has 19 top-10 World Cup finishes ... four-time national champ ('01 DH, '00 SG, '96 GS, '95 GS) ... was water and snow skiing at the age of 3 in the Lake Tahoe area ... was '93 world Jet-Ski champ before deciding to focus on just ski racing.

ERIK SCHLOPY

Height, Weight: 5' 10", 185 lb
Birthdate, Place: Aug. 21, 1972, Buffalo, N.Y.
Hometown: Park City, Utah
Year on U.S. Team: 7th
School: Burke Mountain Academy
Events: Slalom, Giant Slalom

Highlights: '94 Olympian (GS) ... retired after '95 season to race professionally, but returned to World Cup racing in '99 ... in '01, earned best U.S. men's GS World Cup results since Phil Mahre in '83 ... 3rd in overall '01 World Cup GS standings, earning two silver medals ... five–time national champ since '92, including '01 SG and SL crowns ... started skiing at age 2 at Kissing Bridge, outside Buffalo ... was Eastern junior champ at 14, J-1 slalom/GS champ at 16, and a U.S. Ski Team member at 18.

ALPINE (Women)

KIRSTEN CLARK

Height, Weight: 5' 6", 145 lb

Birthdate, Place: April 23, 1977, Portland, Maine

Hometown: Raymond, Maine

Year on U.S. Team: 8th

Club: Carrabassett Valley Academy/Sugarloaf

Events: Downhill, Giant Slalom, Super G

Highlights: '98 Olympian (CO, DH) … had first World Cup win in '01 (DH) for her 5th top-10 career finish … also had two top-10s at the '01 World Championships … has six national titles ('98, '99, '00, '01 DH; '00 SG; '96 CO), including a USA-record (male or female) four straight DH wins … was on skis at age 3 and racing by age 7 … '94 Junior Olympic champ and '97 Nor Am GS champ.

MEGAN GERETY

Height, Weight: 5' 7", 155 lb

Birthdate, Place: Oct. 14, 1971, Anchorage, Alaska

Hometown: Anchorage, Alaska

Year on U.S. Team: 12th

Club: Mt. Alyeska/Sun Valley

Events: Downhill, Super G

Highlights: '92 (injured in training) and '94 Olympian (DH) … leg injuries sidelined her during '98 … 4th in '01 Worlds SG and 5th in '96 DH … seventh in '99 World Cup Finals DH … 5th in first World Cup DH ('91) … lives in Jackson Hole, Wyo., with boyfriend and Olympic medalist Tommy Moe.

KRISTINA KOZNICK

Height, Weight: 5' 7", 156 lb

Birthdate, Place: Nov. 24, 1975, Minneapolis, Minn.

Hometown: Burnsville, Minn.

School: Evansville

Events: Slalom, Giant Slalom

Highlights: '98 Olympian (SL) ... skied in her first World Cup at age 15 and has earned four slalom wins since (two in '00, one each in '98 and '99) ... won four consecutive U.S. slalom titles (1995–98) ... 2nd in '98 final World Cup SL standings ... holds eight junior titles (3 GS, 2 SL, 2 SG, 1 DH).

CAROLINE LALIVE

Height, Weight: 5' 5", 137 lb

Birthdate, Place: Aug. 10, 1979, Truckee, Calif.

Hometown: Steamboat Springs, Colo.

Year on U.S. Team: 6th

School: Colorado

Club: SSWSC

Events: Downhill, Combined, Slalom, Giant Slalom, Super G

Highlights: '98 Olympian (7th CO) ... earned World Cup points in all five events the past two seasons, including two silver medals (CO) in '01 and a bronze ('00 GS) ... won two '00 U.S. titles (SL, CO) ... '99 World junior combined champ ... Born in the U.S. and raised in Switzerland, began skiing at age 2 ... a top soccer player and ski racer in Steamboat, but chose skiing when family moved to Oregon in '95.

JONNA MENDES

Height, Weight: 5' 9", 160 lb
Birthdate, Place: March 31, 1979, Santa Cruz, Calif.
Hometown: Heavenly, Calif.
Year on U.S. Team: 6th
School: UCal (extension)
Club: Heavenly SEF
Events: Downhill, Combined, Giant Slalom, Super G

Highlights: '98 Olympian (CO, DH, SG) ... earned first World Cup top-10 (9th CO) and first U.S. title (GS) in '01, then broke a bone in her right foot three gates shy of the SL finish line (and CO gold medal) ... '99 and '98 DH silver medalist at World Junior Championships ... started skiing at 4 when family moved from California's coast to Lake Tahoe.

KATIE MONAHAN

Height, Weight: 5' 7", 144 lb
Birthdate, Place: Nov. 9, 1972, Aspen, Colo.
Hometown: Aspen
Year on U.S. Team: 9th
School: Colorado
Club: Ski Sunlight
Events: Downhill, Combined, Giant Slalom, Super G

Highlights: '98 Olympian (DH, SG)... 3rd in '99 SG at St. Moritz ... '99 marked her first World Cup top-10 and first two U.S. titles (SG, CO) ... sidelined by two years of injuries, is determined to be a contender again ... high school valedictorian ... accepted at Dartmouth, but has put school on hold until racing career is finished.

SARAH SCHLEPER

Height, Weight: 5' 4", 140 lb
Birthdate, Place: Feb. 19, 1979, Glenwood Springs, Colo.
Hometown: Vail, Colo.
Year on U.S. Team: 6th
School: Vail Valley Academy
Events: Slalom, Giant Slalom

Highlights: '98 Olympian (SL) ... World Cup podium in SL and GS in '01 ... first top-10 World Cup in '00 (SL) ... two-time U.S. champ ('01 SL, '98 GS) ... '97 World Junior SL silver medalist ... birthday gift of skis at age 2 got her started in the sport ... started racing at 11 and was 16 at first World Cup ... broken leg in '99 caused her to miss World Championships in Vail.

PICABO STREET

Height, Weight: 5' 7", 162 lb
Birthdate, Place: April 3, 1971, Triumph, Idaho
Hometown: Park City, Utah
Year on U.S. Team: 14th
School: Wood River H.S.
Events: Downhill, Super G

Highlights: '98 Olympic SG champion, '94 Olympic DH silver medalist ... back after two seasons away while recovering from post-Olympic leg injuries ... '96 Worlds champ ... '95 and '96 World Cup DH champ (only U.S. skier to win consecutive World Cup titles) ... '93 Worlds CO silver medalist ... '96 Worlds SG bronze medalist ... four-time national champ ('96 DH, '96 SG, '94 DH, '93 SG) ... started skiing at age 5 and was racing by age 7.

CROSS-COUNTRY (Men)

TORIN KOOS

Height, Weight: 6' 2", 175 lb
Birthdate, Place: July 7, 1980, Minneapolis, Minn.
Hometown: Leavenworth, Wash.
Year on U.S. Team: 1st
School: Utah
Club: Leavenworth Winter Sports Club

Highlights: Competed at '01 Worlds, finishing 29th in sprint freestyle ... 11th in first World Cup race in '01 at Olympic Trials in Soldier Hollow, Utah ... nicknamed "Thunder" ... father was a member of the U.S. Biathlon Team in the '70s ... started cross-country racing at age 12 ... earned a running scholarship and then made the University of Utah ski team.

MARCUS NASH

Height, Weight: 5' 10", 160 lb
Birthdate, Place: April 1, 1971, Bristol, England
Hometown: Fryeburg, Maine
Year on U.S. Team: 8th
School: Utah ('95)
Club: Auburn (Calif.) Ski Club

Highlights: Two-time Olympian ('98, '94) ... nine-time U.S. champion (3 in '00, 3 in '99, 2 in '98, 1 in '97) ... gold medalist in '00 Goodwill Games 2-man sprint ... broke his left shoulder in spring of '01 ... family moved from England to Canada and then to Maine when he was 5 ... U.S. citizen since he was 18 ... earned his private pilot's license and hopes to fly commercial planes when he retires from racing.

CARL SWENSON
Height, Weight: 5' 9", 145 lb
Birthdate, Place: April 20, 1970, Corvallis, Ore.
Hometown: Boulder, Colo.
Year on U.S. Team: 3rd
School: Dartmouth ('93)
Club: The Factory Team

Highlights: '94 Olympian ... had best international results in his career in '01, including a 16th-place World Cup on the Olympic trails and a 21st place at World Championships ... four-time U.S. champ, including '01 sprint title ... began alpine skiing at Oregon's Mount Bachelor before moving to New Hampshire and switching to cross-country ... two-time captain of ski team at Dartmouth, where he majored in government.

JUSTIN WADSWORTH
Height, Weight: 6' 1", 175 lb
Birthdate, Place: Aug. 14, 1968, La Jolla, Calif.
Hometown: Bend, Ore.
Year on U.S. Team: 8th
School: Central Oregon Community College
Club: XC Oregon

Highlights: '94 and '98 Olympian ... earned best U.S. cross-country result since '84 with an 8th-place '01 World Cup 30-km freestyle finish on the Olympic course at Soldier Hollow ... trained with Norwegian men's team in the summer of '01 ...'00 Goodwill Games two-man sprint relay champ ... four-time U.S. champ (2 in '01, 2 in '95) ... began skiing at age 4, switched to cross-country at 12 ... used to train in the summer with the U.S. junior rowing team ... has endured numerous injuries, including a broken back in '97.

CROSS-COUNTRY (Women)

NINA KEMPPEL
Height, Weight: 5' 10", 140 lb
Birthdate, Place: Oct. 14, 1970, Boulder, Colo.
Hometown: Anchorage, Alaska
Year on U.S. Team: 13th
School: Dartmouth ('92)
Club: Nordic Ski Association of Anchorage Gold 2002

Highlights: '92, '94, '98 Olympian ... trying to become first U.S. female cross-country skier to compete in four Olympic Winter Games ... all-time U.S. titleholder with 15 (3 in '01, 4 in '00, 5 in '99, 1 each in '97, '95, '94) ... earned six top-30 finishes in '01 (3 each at World Championships, World Cups) ... grew up in Alaska, skiing, running, and swimming ... climbed Alaska's Denali (Mt. McKinley) with her father in summer of '95 and has spent two off-seasons as part-time ranger at the base camp.

WENDY WAGNER
Height, Weight: 5' 4", 138 lb
Birthdate, Place: Oct. 31, 1973, Salt Lake City, Utah
Hometown: Park City, Utah
Year on U.S. Team: 3rd
School: Western State ('96)
Club: Gold 2002

Highlights: Earned her first World Cup points in '01 and had two top-30 finishes at '01 Worlds ... '98 5-km classical champ ... started skiing at age 3 and racing by 7th grade ... also competed in gymnastics and volleyball when she was younger ... nickname is "Wags."

FREESTYLE (Men)

ERIC BERGOUST
Height, Weight: 6' 0", 165 lb
Birthdate, Place: Aug. 27, 1969, Missoula, Mont.
Hometown: Missoula
Year on U.S. Team: 11th
Club: Globalizers

Highlights: '98 Olympic, '99 Worlds, and '01 World Cup aerials champion ... current world record holder, with three of the highest aerials scores in history ... '00 Goodwill Games champion ... '97 Worlds silver medalist ... has 18 top-3 World Cup finishes, including 13 wins, going into '02 season ... has three U.S. titles ('00, '97, '96) ... originally wanted to be a stuntman or fighter pilot, but discovered freestyle aerial skiing during an '85 ESPN broadcast ... also a '94 Olympian ... nickname is "Bergy" ... has his own web site at http://www.airbergy.com/.

BRIAN CURRUTT
Height, Weight: 5' 8", 160 lb
Birthdate, Place: April 11, 1974, Cleveland, Ohio
Hometown: Park City, Utah
Year on U.S. Team: 6th
School: Utah

Highlights: Earned four more top-10 World Cup finishes in '01, including a 3rd place in Heavenly, Calif. ... '01 national aerials bronze medalist ... was 4th in World Cup standings in '99 ... nickname is "Curdog" ... started skiing at age 5 and took up aerials in the early '90s.

TOBY DAWSON

Height, Weight: 5' 7", 155 lb
Birthdate, Place: Nov. 30, 1978, South Korea
Hometown: Vail, Colo.
Year on U.S. Team: 4th
School: Fort Lewis State
Club: Team Summit

Highlights: Earned first World Cup moguls win in March '01 and also earned a 3rd place in '01 ... competed in first World Cup in '99 and has risen quickly since then ... 3rd at '01 nationals in moguls ... adopted at age 3 and tried out first skis a year later in Vail ... raced alpine when he was 6, before switching to freestyle at age 12.

EVAN DYBVIG

Height, Weight: 6' 4", 200 lb
Birthdate, Place: July 29, 1975, Hanover, N.H.
Hometown: Tunbridge, Vt.
Year on U.S. Team: 8th
School: Colorado
Club: Team Breckenridge

Highlights: '98 Olympian ... two '01 World Cup podiums, six in his career ... 6th in moguls at '01 Worlds ... '00 and '94 U.S. moguls champ ... has been 2nd last two years in World Cups on the Olympic course at Deer Valley, Utah ... one of a few competitors who can perform 720s (two full spins) ... started skiing at age 7 and competing at 10.

JERRY GROSSI

Height, Weight: 5' 5", 175 lb
Birthdate, Place: April 23, 1974, Chicago
Hometown: Park City, Utah
Year on U.S. Team: 3rd

Highlights: Earned his first World Cup podium in '01, opening the season with 2nd place at Mt. Buller, Australia … had four more top-10 World Cup finishes in '01 …6th at '01 Worlds in aerials … '01 season was cut short when he broke his right femur in a dirt bike accident … was an all-conference high school diver who didn't start skiing until age 13 … '96 and '97 Nor Am aerials champ … skied both moguls and aerials until '99.

JOE PACK

Height, Weight: 5' 10", 163 lb
Birthdate, Place: April 10, 1978, Eugene, Ore.
Hometown: Park City, Utah
Year on U.S. Team: 6th
School: Utah

Highlights: Aerials bronze medalist at '01 and '99 Worlds … earned his third World Cup win in '01 … had six top-5 World Cup finishes in '01 … '01 and '99 U.S. aerials champ … '96 World Juniors champ … missed '98 Olympic Team berth when he tore his ACL just before the season start … converted from ski jumping to aerials at age 12 … grew up in New Hampshire.

TRAVIS RAMOS

Height, Weight: 5' 10", 167 lb
Birthdate, Place: Feb. 22, 1979, Lake Tahoe, Calif.
Hometown: South Lake Tahoe, Calif.
Year on U.S. Team: 6th
Club: Squaw Valley Ski Team

Highlights: Won his first World Cup in January '01 ... added two more top-10 World Cup finishes in '01 ... broke his left ankle before World Cup Finals, but still competed, placing 11th ... skipped '01 U.S. nationals.

RYAN RILEY

Height, Weight: 5' 9", 155 lb
Birthdate, Place: May 15, 1979, St. Charles, Mo.
Hometown: Steamboat Springs, Colo.
Year on U.S. Team: 4th
School: Whiteman School
Club: Steamboat Springs WSC

Highlights: Earned three top-5 World Cup moguls finishes in '01 ... reigning U.S. moguls champ from '01 ... '00 Goodwill Games silver dual moguls and bronze moguls medalist ... '99 national duals champ ... started skiing when his family moved to Colorado in the late '80s ... '98 Nor Am moguls champ ... eight wins in '97 earned him the Rocky Mountain Division moguls title ... plans to attend Harvard, starting in Fall '02.

BRITT SWARTLEY

Height, Weight: 5' 10", 165 lb
Birthdate, Place: Aug. 3, 1971, Lansdale, Pa.
Hometown: Blue Bell, Pa.
Year on U.S. Team: 8th
Club: Waterville Valley Academy

Highlights: '98 Olympian, placing 5th in aerials … 3rd at '00 Deer Valley World Cup … '00 Goodwill Games aerials silver medalist … has eight World Cup podiums going into '02 season … '98 World Cup win (Tignes, France) …'94 U.S. aerials champ … opened '01 season with 4th- and 7th-place World Cups, but ruptured his right ACL in November to end his season … started alpine skiing at age 12, then took up aerials after seeing a tape of World Cup aerials coverage on ESPN … has a pilot's license and likes to fly single-engine aircraft … also likes surfing.

FREESTYLE (Women)

SHANNON BAHRKE
Height, Weight: 5' 4", 120 lb
Birthdate, Place: Nov. 7, 1980, Reno, Nev.
Hometown: Tahoe City, Calif.
Year on U.S. Team: 4th
Club: Squaw Valley Ski Team

Highlights: '01 U.S. dual moguls champ … six top-10 World Cup finishes in '01 and 15 career top-10s … 2nd in '00 World Cup moguls and '99 World Cup dual moguls, both in Madarao, Japan … 5th in moguls at '01 U.S. championships after winning bronze medal in '00 …5th in duals at '00 Goodwill Games … started skiing at age 3 … skied combined before concentrating on moguls … also played soccer and softball, ran track, and played trumpet in symphonic and jazz bands in high school.

ANN BATTELLE
Height, Weight: 5' 9", 160 lb
Birthdate, Place: Jan. 18, 1968, Yonkers, N.Y.
Hometown: Steamboat Springs, Colo.
Year on U.S. Team: 10th
Club: Steamboat Springs WSC

Highlights: Three-time Olympian ('92, '94, '98) … two-time World Cup ('00, '99) and '99 moguls world champion … '99 Worlds bronze medalist in dual moguls … dislocated her left shoulder and broke the shoulder socket in a September '00 training camp crash… recovered quickly, competing again in January '01, earning top-10 finishes in four of five World Cups she entered … six-time U.S. champ ('99 M, '99 DM, '98 DM, '97 M, '95 M, '93 M) … '00 Goodwill Games dual moguls champ and moguls silver medalist …also played soccer and softball and competed in gymnastics in high school and soccer at Middlebury.

EMILY COOK

Height, Weight: 5' 3", 120 lb
Birthdate, Place: July 1, 1979, Boston
Hometown: Belmont, Mass.
Year on U.S. Team: 5th
School: Utah
Club: Carrabassett Valley Academy

Highlights: First World Cup podium (3rd) and U.S. title in
'01 ... started '01 season on "C" Team, then won two selection
events, earned 3rd at the World Cup on Olympic course in Deer
Valley and added three top-10 finishes ... had five World Cup
top-10s overall in '01 ... raised by her father after her mother
died when Emily was 2 ... was a diver and gymnast before
committing to skiing full-time ... part time gymnastics coach in
Park City in preseason.

HANNAH HARDAWAY

Height, Weight: 5' 7", 135 lb
Birthdate, Place: Dec. 10, 1978, Concord, N.H.
Hometown: Moultonborough, N.H.
Year on U.S. Team: 7th
School: Cornell
Club: Team Summit

Highlights: Two-time defending U.S. moguls champ ('01, '00)
and '00 dual champ ... first two World Cup wins and four
podiums in '01 ... entering '02, had six top-10 World Cup finishes
... '97 World Juniors champ ... sidelined by knee surgery in '98
and '99 ... began competitive skiing (for Killington, Vt., freestyle
team) at age 12 ... a senior at Cornell University, majoring in
business management and marketing.

BRENDA PETZOLD

Height, Weight: 5' 6", 132 lb
Birthdate, Place: Aug. 6, 1973, Lawrence, Mass.
Hometown: Andover, Mass.
Year on U.S. Team: 7th
School: Union College
Club: Carrabassett Valley Academy

Highlights: Had career-best 4th place at '01 opening World Cup in Australia ... had four more World Cup top-10s in '01 ...her '01 season ended in February when she fractured her right collarbone while training and missed '01 World Cup finals and U.S. championships ... U.S. aerials silver medalist in '00 ... bronze medalist at '00 Goodwill Games ... is a certified scuba diver ... older sister, Sharon, won '93 Worlds silver medal in ballet and bronze at '92 Olympic Winter Games when it was a demo event.

NORDIC COMBINED

MATT DAYTON
Height, Weight: 5' 10", 150 lb
Birthdate, Place: Aug. 24, 1977, Fairplay, Colo.
Hometown: Breckenridge, Colo.
Year on U.S. Team: 2nd
School: Summit H.S. Nordic/SSWSC

Highlights: Won World Cup-B event and earned first World Cup top-10 in '01 … had six World Cup top-30s in '01 … 5th at '01 U.S. nationals and 2nd in '99 … parents own Breckenridge Nordic Center, and he grew up on cross-country skis … started jumping when he was almost 19.

BILL DEMONG
Height, Weight: 5' 10", 150 lb
Birthdate, Place: March 29, 1980, Saranac Lake, N.Y.
Hometown: Vermontville, N.Y.
Year on U.S. Team: 3rd
Club: SSWSC

Highlights: '98 Olympian (17 years old) …earned first World Cup top-10 finish (9th) in '01 … had seven top-15 results in '01, finishing 16th overall … was 2nd in jumping and 11th overall in World Cup in Steamboat Springs … starting skiing at 6 years, jumping at 10.

KRISTOFFER ERICHSEN

Height, Weight: 5' 11", 155 lb
Birthdate, Place: Feb. 11, 1978, Rapid City, S.D.
Hometown: Steamboat Springs, Colo.
Year on U.S. Team: 3rd
Club: SSWSC

Highlights: '98 Olympian (DNC) ... grew up in Norway, has dual citizenship, but was released by Norwegian Ski Federation in '95 to ski for the U.S. ... '96 Norwegian junior champion, '95 bronze medalist ... 4th in Nordic combined and 9th in ski jumping on both hills (90 m, 120 m) at '01 U.S. championships.

NATHAN GERHART

Height, Weight: 6' 4", 175 lb
Birthdate, Place: March 20, 1983,
Steamboat Springs, Colo.
Hometown: Steamboat Springs, Colo.
Year on U.S. Team: 1st
School: Steamboat Springs H.S.
Club: SSWSC

Highlights: '99 U.S. championships bronze medalist in Nordic combined and 5th-place jumper on 90-m hill ... placed 5th in World Cup-B sprint event before '01 Junior Worlds ... three-time World Juniors skier ... J2 Junior Olympic individual champ in '98 and '99 ... '00 J1 national champ ... starting skiing at age 3, racing alpine at 6, jumping a few years later.

JED HINKLEY

Height, Weight: 5' 10", 155 lb
Birthdate, Place: June 5, 1981, Concord, N.H.
Hometown: Andover, N.H.
Year on U.S. Team: 1st
School: Proctor Academy
Club: Andover Outing Club/SSWSC

Highlights: Placed 8th in sprint at '01 World Junior Championships, to earn World Cup starting spot for 2001–02 season ... member of gold-medal U.S. team at '99 Junior Worlds and silver-medal team at '00 Junior Worlds ... 7th in Nordic combined at '01 U.S. nationals ... son of a Nordic combined skier ... started skiing at age 3, alpine racing at 6, and combined at 12.

TODD LODWICK

Height, Weight: 5' 9", 140 lb
Birthdate, Place: Nov. 21, 1976, Steamboat Springs, Colo.
Hometown: Steamboat Springs, Colo.
Year on U.S. Team: 9th
School: Steamboat Springs H.S.
Club: SSWSC

Highlights: '98, '94 Olympian ... 4th in World Cup in '00, '98 ... four World Cup wins (one each in '01 and '96; two in '98) ... prior to '02 season, had 12 World Cup podiums ... eight-time U.S. champ (5 combined, 3 jumping) ... member of 4th-place U.S. team at '95 World Championships ... won his first international meet in '93 to open the International Cup (World Cup-B season) ... recently married.

JOHNNY SPILLANE

Height, Weight: 6' 1", 145 lb

Birthdate, Place: Nov. 24, 1980,
Steamboat Springs, Colo.

Hometown: Steamboat Springs, Colo.

Year on U.S. Team: 2nd

School: Whiteman School

Club: SSWSC

Highlights: '98 Olympian (DNC) ... won and placed 2nd at two '01 World Cup-B events on '02 Olympic course at Soldier Hollow, Utah ... top U.S. sprinter (14th) at '01 World Championships ... started skiing at age 2, but didn't take up jumping until 10 or 11.

SKI JUMPING

ALAN ALBORN
Height, Weight: 5' 11", 130 lb
Birthdate, Place: Dec. 13, 1980, Anchorage, Alaska
Hometown: Anchorage
Year on U.S. Team: 3rd
School: Home-schooled
Club: Alaska Jumping Club

Highlights: '98 Olympian ... had career-best 11th place in World Cup Finals ... won U.S. 120-m championship in '01, for his second large-hill national title ('99) ... '01 national runner-up on 90-m hill ... set U.S. distance mark of 210 meters in '01 in training in Obersdorf, Germany ... started '01 season with a bad right ankle sprain ... had five top-35 World Cup or Worlds results in '01 ... started skiing at age 2 and jumping at age 9 ... was only 17 when he made the '98 Olympic Team ... Alan has a pilot's license, as well as his own single-engine plane.

CLINT JONES
Height, Weight: 5' 9", 120 lb
Birthdate, Place: Oct. 5, 1984, Monroe, Wis.
Hometown: Steamboat Springs, Colo.
Year on U.S. Team: 2nd
Club: Steamboat Springs WSC

Highlights: Became youngest U.S. champion in any skiing discipline in March 2000, winning the large-hill (120-m) title in his hometown ... was 5th (90 m) and 6th (120 m) at '01 U.S. national championships ... high school junior ... learned to alpine ski first and then tried jumping when he was about 5 years old after his older brother (Robbie) started.

SNOWBOARDING (Men)

RICKY BOWER
Height, Weight: 5' 8", 170 lb
Birthdate, Place: Oct. 20, 1977, Park City, Utah
Hometown: Park City
Year on U.S. Team: 5th
School: Park City Winter School
Stance: Regular

Highlights: Four '01 Grand Prix top-10 finishes ... '99 FIS world halfpipe champ, 12th at '01 Worlds ... four FIS World Cup top-10s in '00, including silver medal in Berchtesgaden, Germany, World Cup ... 4th in halfpipe at '01 U.S. nationals ... 4th at '00 Goodwill Games in halfpipe.

TOMMY CZESCHIN
Height, Weight: 5' 9", 145 lb
Birthdate, Place: June 15, 1979, Mammoth Lakes, Calif.
Hometown: Mammoth Lakes
Year on U.S. Team: 7th
Stance: Goofy

Highlights: Two-time medalist in halfpipe at X Games ('01 silver, '00 bronze) ... '01 World Cup halfpipe champ in Asahikawa, Japan ... silver medalist at '00 Gravity Games and Goodwill Games ... '01 and '00 silver medalist at U.S. Snowboard Grand Prix ... 3rd at '01 U.S. championships ... blew out his left knee in April 2000 at Sims World Snowboarding Championships, but has come back strong ... one of the few riders who has completed 1080s (three full spins) in the superpipe competition ... started skiing at age 3 ... taught himself to snowboard when he was 10 and started competing at 16.

JEFF GREENWOOD
Height, Weight: 5' 7", 165 lb
Birthdate, Place: May 15, 1975, Hartford, Conn.
Hometown: Granby, Conn.
Year on U.S. Team: 7th
School: Carrabassett Valley Academy
Stance: Regular

Highlights: '96 World GS champion ... three-time U.S. slalom champ ('01, '99, '97) and '97 GS national champ ... sidelined for part of '01 season with wrist injury ... 2nd at '01 U.S. Snowboard Grand Prix in parallel GS ... two World Cup GS wins ('96, '98) and nine career World Cup top-5 performances ... double gold medalist at '95 World University Games ... recreational skier until he was 12 ... took up riding after a friend bought a snowboard while they were on vacation together ... works at Home Depot in the Olympic Job Opportunities Program.

ROB KINGWILL
Height, Weight: 5' 9", 160 lb
Birthdate, Place: June 25, 1975, Durango, Colo.
Hometown: Jackson, Wyo.
Year on U.S. Team: 7th
School: Montana State
Stance: Regular

Highlights: First in '00 Grand Prix HP standings ... bronze at '00 Goodwill Games ... '00 World Cup win at Tignes ... seven top-3 World Cup performances since 1976 ... silver at '00 Gravity Games, bronze at '00 Goodwill Games in halfpipe ... '98 U.S. Open halfpipe champ ... nickname is "Kinger" ... barely missed making the '98 Olympic squad.

ANTON POGUE

Height, Weight: 6' 2", 192 lb
Birthdate, Place: June 20, 1968, Sunnyvale, Calif.
Hometown: Hood River, Ore.
Year on U.S. Team: 7th
School: Nevada
Stance: Goofy

Highlights: Parallel slalom bronze medalist at '01 FIS Worlds ... slalom bronze at '97 FIS Worlds ... two-time ('00, '94) U.S. SL champ ... has 10 career FIS World Cup top-5 finishes, including two podiums in '00 ... knee injury and torn rotator cuff limited his '01 season ... was an All-America ski racer for Nevada-Reno, before taking a couple of years off ...'91 U.S. Amateur Snowboard Association slalom champ ... married to ex-World Cup rider Jeanne Pogue, who is now a physical therapist.

SETH WESCOTT

Height, Weight: 6' 2", 181 lb
Birthdate, Place: June 28, 1976, Durham, N.C.
Hometown: Farmington, Maine
Year on U.S. Team: 3rd
School: Western State
Stance: Goofy

Highlights: '01 X Games snowboardcross (SBX) bronze medalist ... earned three World Cup top-10s in '01 to bring career total to seven ... '00 U.S. SBX champ ... two ISF podiums in '00 ... hopes the 2006 Olympic Winter Games will include snowboardcross, his specialty ... recovering from torn right ACL sustained at Feb. 28 World Cup in '01 ... played soccer and ran track in high school ... also skateboards, mountain bikes, and kayaks ... hopes to build his own home someday on 13 acres he owns near Sugarloaf.

SNOWBOARDING (Women)

GRETCHEN BLEILER
Height, Weight: 5' 4", 120 lb
Birthdate, Place: April 10, 1981, Toledo, Ohio
Hometown: Snowmass Village, Colo.
Year on U.S. Team: 2nd
Stance: Goofy

Highlights: First career FIS World Cup win in '01 (halfpipe) … first career Triple Crown podium (3rd) in '01 … 5th at '01 Sims World Snowboarding Championships, 11th at '01 FIS Worlds in halfpipe … 2nd at '01 U.S. championships and 3rd at '01 U.S. Open … added a "McTwist" to her trick repertoire last season … started riding after moving to Colorado when she was about 14 … mountain bikes in off-season.

TRICIA BYRNES
Height, Weight: 5' 7", 145 lb
Birthdate, Place: Nov. 18, 1974, Greenwich, Conn.
Hometown: Stratton Mountain, Vt.
Year on U.S. Team: 4th
School: St. Michael's College (Vt./'98)
Stance: Goofy

Highlights: Won '01 Grand Prix halfpipe title with two wins … two '01 Triple Crown podiums (1st, 2nd) … 14 career FIS World Cup wins … '00 Goodwill Games HP champ … third at '01 Sims World Snowboarding Championships (HP) … has 13 ISF podiums … started skiing at age 4, riding in 1989 … was a double major (English, psychology) at St. Michael's College.

KELLY CLARK

Height, Weight: 5' 5", 130 lb
Birthdate, Place: July 26, 1983, Newport, R.I.
Hometown: Mount Snow, Vt.
Year on U.S. Team: 2nd
School: Brattleboro Union H.S./ Mount Snow Academy
Stance: Regular

Highlights: '01 U.S. halfpipe and snowboardcross champ ... earned first Triple Crown and FIS World Cup victories in '01 ... '00 World Juniors halfpipe champ ... 9th at '01 FIS Worlds ... had three top-3 finishes at '01 Grand Prix events ... silver medalist at '01 Sims World Snowboarding Championships, '00 Goodwill Games ... four-year tennis player in high school ... has been a surfer for five years.

STACIA HOOKOM

Height, Weight: 5' 3", 135 lb
Birthdate, Place: July 22, 1975, Denver, Colo.
Hometown: Vail, Colo.
Year on U.S. Team: 8th
School: Colorado
Stance: Goofy

Highlights: Won '01 parallel GS at Grand Prix in Breckenridge, Colo. ... two top-10 World Cups in '01 ... has eight career FIS World Cup podiums entering '02 season ... 8th at '01, '97, and '96 FIS Worlds in parallel GS ... silver medalist in PSL at '01 U.S. nationals ... 3rd in SG at '00 Goodwill Games ... was alpine ski racer in high school and took up snowboarding in '89 when she had free lessons in Vail ... started competitive riding at age 17.

SONDRA VAN ERT

Height, Weight: 5' 9", 145 lb
Birthdate, Place: March 9, 1964, Des Moines, Iowa
Hometown: Ketchum, Idaho
Year on U.S. Team: 8th
School: Utah ('89)
Stance: Regular

Highlights: '98 Olympian (12th, GS) ... '97 World GS champ ... won '01 Okemo (Vt.) Grand Prix in parallel GS ... competed in three snowboardcross events in '01, finishing 13th in Tignes, France ... three-time FIS Worlds bronze medalist ('99 GS, '96 GS, '96 PSL) ... seven top-10 World Cup finishes in '01 ... two World Cup wins and four podiums in '00... '00 Goodwill Games SG champ ... 10 U.S. titles (1993–2000) ... has been a member of both U.S. Ski and U.S. Snowboard teams ... born in Iowa, but raised in Utah mountains and started skiing at age 3, competing at 10 ... retired from skiing in mid-'80s to go to University of Utah ... while rehabbing her knee in '90, she saw others snowboarding ... she took it up when she was 25 and began to compete at age 29.

3

Getting Started

Skiing and snowboarding are equal opportunity sports, suitable for anyone from about the age of three or older. They are a wonderful way to remain active, meet others, see new places, enjoy time with the family, and much more. If you're athletic and you like biking, swimming, roller skating, ice skating, skateboarding, surfing, or water skiing, you have valuable experience already. You know your natural balance, and you are probably well coordinated. In all likelihood, you are in good physical condition, with sufficient muscle strength (especially in your legs), and have confidence in yourself and your body. All these qualities equip you to be a good skier or snowboarder.

Learning to Ski or Snowboard

Your nearest public library is a good place to start to learn more about skiing or snowboarding if you're a beginner. It usually has books covering the major sports and may have videos available for a small fee. Read, learn the vocabulary, and find out what equipment a beginner needs. Taking a few inexpensive lessons from a certified skiing or snowboarding instructor will give you a "feel" for the equipment and help you decide if this is a sport you enjoy. Also, you'll learn to ski or snowboard correctly and won't develop bad habits that can be difficult to unlearn later on. Lessons with a group on the beginners' slopes can be fun and provide extra help as you watch and learn together with other members of your group. When snow is not available, basic skiing can be learned on a ski ramp covered with indoor-outdoor carpet. Even as you become more confident on the slopes, taking additional lessons can only help improve your technique and enjoyment of the sport.

To find a certified ski or snowboard instructor, you might contact your school's physical education department, the YMCA or YWCA, or your community's parks and recreation department. You can also visit the web site of the U.S. Ski and Snowboard Association (USSA), the national governing body for skiing and snowboarding in the U.S., to find links and contact information for USSA regional offices and other recommended resources and sites (http://www.usskiteam.com/). Local ski shops might have information about skiing areas nearby, and knowledgeable store personnel should be able to point you in the right direction. The business section of your telephone book can be a resource, too. Look under the headings for "skiing," "ski equipment," "ski pro shops," "snowboards," and/or "ski schools." If you have a computer and access to the World Wide Web, don't overlook this source of instant information. Also see the list of organizations and web sites in Chapter 12 of this book.

Collect as much information as possible. Some ski resorts offer ski and/or snowboard packages that include basic lessons, lift tickets, and equipment rentals. In many areas, you can also purchase discounted lift and lesson tickets in advance through a local ski shop, grocery, or convenience store. Until you're certain that this is a sport you want to pursue, rent equipment the first few times you ski or snowboard.

First Lessons

Beginning skiers should spend some time standing and watching other skiers. To avoid getting cold, beginners should do their watching on an east-facing slope in the morning and a west-facing slope in the afternoon, to take advantage of the sun's warmth.

If you're a beginner, a tow up the mountain is the easiest way to get to the top and will give you more time to ski or snowboard. If possible, ask about tows and slopes in advance. Many ski resorts provide maps of their areas and will send you this information in advance. You can also check with the local ski and snowboard shops to see if they can provide more information.

Types of Snow

Snow can be categorized in several ways. These include:

- **Freshly groomed snow**—great for *schussing*, or speeding downhill on a path along the fall line.

- **Fresh powder snow**—light and dry. The skiing technique used on powder is different from the technique used on groomed trails. The skis should float through powder, and your weight must be balanced on both skis.

- **Spring snow**—heavy and slushy, especially after a warm day. This can make skiing difficult.

- **Icy**—conditions can be treacherous.

Carrying Your Equipment

Getting from the parking lot or ski rental shop to the lift requires that you carry your skis, snowboard, and other gear. The following procedure is recommended for carrying skis:

- Stand your skis on their tails with the bottoms together.

- Hold them together at their tips and tails with an inexpensive, stretchy ski strap.

- Carry your skis over one shoulder with the tips in front and pointed down far enough so that the tails are up and out of the way, especially of the people behind you.

- Use your other hand to carry your poles, which are good for steadying you as you walk in ski boots.

If it is too crowded to carry your skis over your shoulder, hold them in front of you, with the tips up and the tails down.

Up the Slope on a Tow

Tows are a fast way up the slope and increase the amount of time you'll have to ski or snowboard. A T-bar tow usually holds two skiers. It pulls you uphill as you lean back with your skis in the track (keep your knees flexed), your ski poles in one hand, and the bar in the other. At the top of the hill, you release the bar and move to the runout area to get out of the way of the skiers coming up behind you.

T-bar lifts take one skier at a time, and chairlifts (for steeper, longer slopes) are usually for two, three, or four skiers or snowboarders. Chairlifts are similar to an amusement park ride, complete with a metal safety bar that holds skiers in position.

Gondolas carry up to six skiers and their poles; skis are stowed in a rack on the outside of the gondola. Allow extra time for putting on your skis at the top.

Putting on Skis

Each ski has an outside edge and an inside edge. Edges are the sharp metal borders on your skis. The outside edge of your uphill ski faces the ski slope when you are standing across the fall line, the steepest path down a slope; at the same time, the outside edge of your downhill ski faces down the slope. When you are skiing down the fall line, the outside edges run parallel to the line. Skiers dig in their edges when they want to slow down, brake, walk up a slope, or turn.

The technique for putting on skis varies depending on whether you are on flat ground or sloping ground.

Flat Ground

On flat ground, do the following:

- Stick ski poles in the snow close enough to reach easily.
- Stick skis on their tails in the snow and remove straps that hold them together.
- Check that skis are undamaged.
- Put one ski on the snow and check that safety straps are open.
- Remove any snow from the ski boot bottoms.
- Step into bindings toe-first, centering the boot.
- Stomp the heel of the boot into the heel binding. The binding should "click" into place.
- Repeat with the other ski.

Sloping Ground

Use a slightly different approach for sloping ground.

- Find the fall line, the steepest path down any ski slope. It changes direction as you ski, but is always the steepest line.
- Stick poles and skis in the snow on the uphill side (the side closer to the top of the slope) and check for any damage.
- Place the downhill ski (the one closer to the bottom of the slope) at a right angle to the fall line and attach the safety strap to your ankle.

- Step into the bindings and secure them by stomping. Repeat with the uphill ski.

Standing Up

With your skis on and the bindings secured, you're ready to learn how to stand up.

- Move your feet about six inches apart, with your weight evenly balanced toward the front of your skis.
- Press your ankles against the inside of the boot's tongue.
- Bend your knees just enough so they'll be about six inches apart and over the toes of your boots.
- Keep your hips over your feet, not jutting out in back.
- Keep your chin up and look ahead.
- Forget you're on skis; don't look down.
- Lean forward slightly.
- Holding your ski poles, bend your elbows. Your hands will be about as high as your hips and slightly away from your body.
- The ends of your ski poles should angle down to the heel of your ski boot. They should not stick out behind your boots and skis.
- Stay relaxed and get ready for the next move: walking.

Walking

Walking on skis requires more concentration than walking in street shoes on a hard surface. If you get into a rhythm that will give you momentum, you'll move right along. Bend your knees, keep them relaxed, and begin to take short, sliding steps, using your ski poles to guide you on the snow.

- Shift your body weight to the left ski and the right pole, and slide the right ski forward.

- Shift your weight to the right ski and the left pole, and slide the left ski forward.

- Keep the poles close to the tips of your skis when you plant them. Don't reach too far in front.

- Stiff legs and locked knees will lift the ski tips and result in crossed skis.

- Move your feet apart about six inches, with your weight evenly balanced toward the front of your skis.

- Press your ankles against the inside of the boot's tongue.

- Bend your knees just enough so they'll be about six inches apart and over the toes of your boots.

- Keep your hips over your feet, not jutting out in back.

- Keep your chin up and look ahead.

Stopping

The practical approach to stopping is to squat low, sit back, and drag your hands at your sides. The preferred method is the "snowplow."

- Keep your weight even on each ski.

- Lean your feet inward slightly and push the ski tails out. The tips will move toward each other, forming a V that brakes your forward motion.

Your ski tips may cross at first, but this will change as you gain experience.

Turns

There are several types of skiing turns. The easiest are the *step turn* and the *snowplow turn*.

For a step turn:

- With the ski tail on the ground, raise the tip and move the ski sideways.

- Repeat with the other ski.

- Continue, alternating skis, until you are heading in a new direction.

For a snowplow turn:

- Place ski tips close together and ski tails far apart, forming a wedge.

- Lean forward over boots.

- Turn by shifting weight to uphill or downhill ski.

- If the weight is not shifted, a snowplow stop occurs.

At first, practice stops and turns on level ground to gain confidence and a feel for the movements involved. Later, you can learn more advanced techniques, including the sidestep, the herringbone, and how to traverse (move sideways across a slope).

Falling

Every skier falls, even the champions, and you will, too—but that's no reason to get discouraged. Here are several techniques for falling and getting back up:

- If the fall happens while you're going downhill, squat, sit down sideways, or fall to one side. Snow and snow banks make good cushions.

- Don't sit down on your skis—you'll continue right on down the slope and probably hurt yourself or another skier.

- If the fall is in deep snow, get the skis under your body. Then stand up slowly, using your poles for support.

- If the fall is in very deep snow, and you're partly buried, get out of your skis and put one on each side of you. (If you have safety straps, don't detach them or you'll lose your skis!) Then, using your arms, lift yourself up to the snow level and back onto your skis. To stand up, use your poles for support.

Courtesy on the Slopes

A day skiing or snowboarding in the fresh air is a wonderful experience and can be nearly perfect if people follow a few simple courtesies and practice common sense. Basic rules of courtesy include:

- Check all your equipment before getting on the ski lift.

- With rental equipment, be sure the boots fit and the bindings clamp securely.

- Read, understand, and obey all trail marking signs. They are posted for the benefit of all skiers and snowboarders. (Some ski areas do not allow snowboarders on all trails; check the access rules.)

- Stay in control of your speed and direction.

- Ski/snowboard safely; don't endanger others.

- When stopped, move off to the side and don't obstruct the trail or path down a slope.

- Be sure other skiers/snowboarders can see you.

- Report all accidents as soon as possible to the local ski patrol or a ski lift operator.

- Don't leave trash behind; carry it out with you.

4

Alpine and Freestyle Skiing

Alpine skiing is fairly basic. The objective is to ski down a snow-covered course from the top to the bottom. In alpine racing, the skier goes from the top to the bottom of the hill on the assigned course, and the person to reach the bottom in the fastest time wins. There's no waiting for judges or points; it's a race against the clock. Races are timed in increments of .01 second.

Learning Alpine Skiing

Group skiing lessons are the best way to learn. Be sure the instructor is certified so you'll learn correctly, with no bad habits to break later on. Read as much as you can about the sport before your lessons. Then you'll be familiar with the vocabulary and be free to concentrate on getting used to the feel of skis and moving on snow.

For more information on learning the basics of alpine skiing, see Chapter 3, "Getting Started."

Alpine Competitions

From its small beginnings as a single competition at the 1936 Olympic Winter Games, alpine racing has grown to encompass five separate Olympic events: downhill (DH), slalom (SL), giant slalom (GS), super giant slalom or Super G (SG), and combined (slalom and downhill; CO). Each event is held separately for men and women, which doubles the number of competitions. Downhill and Super G are the exciting speed events; slalom and giant slalom are considered "technical" events. All the events use tall poles, the gates that mark the downhill course.

Jed Jacobsohn/ALLSPORT

Chad Fleischer of Team USA leans into the mountain during the men's downhill event at the World Cup Skiing Olympic Course in Snowbasin, Utah.

Downhill (DH)

Speed, speed, and more speed—that's what matters and wins competitions in this popular, exciting event. Skiing downhill is fast and dangerous, a mental and physical challenge that is not for the fainthearted. Champion skiers control their nervous energy and use it to boost their speed (which, at times, can reach between 80 and 90 miles per hour) down the approximately two-mile-long course.

Skiers make two practice runs down the steep, icy slope for the downhill event. Their scores, however, are based on only one run down. For Salt Lake City, planners laid out a course about 3 km long, with a vertical drop of 800–1,000 meters for men (500–800 meters for women), three jumps, and several high-speed turns. The downhill skier tries to stay "tucked," using aerodynamics to increase speed and achieve a winning time. Downhill racers wear skis that have less sidecut and are longer, wider, and stiffer than usual, which gives stability and boosts speed. There are few gates to negotiate, and the skier can reach speeds approaching 90 mph. The best time down the hill wins.

Slalom (SL)

The slalom is a shorter, more technical event than the downhill, with a vertical drop of 140–220 meters for men and 120–200 meters for women. That doesn't mean it's easier than the other events. For men, there are 55–75 speed control gates, consisting of hinged, "breakaway" poles; there are 40–60 gates for the women. Turns must be tight and quick, and skiers must pass close to the gates to control speed, which averages 25 mph. If a gate is missed, the skier is disqualified.

Slalom skis are shorter and have more sidecut, and skiers often wear protective patches on their ski clothes to protect themselves while skiing through the gates. (The gates or poles are hinged and specially designed to first bounce down and out of the way when a skier pushes on them, and then spring back up after the skier passes through them.) Two slalom courses are set side-by-side, and two skiers race at the same time. They change courses after the first run, and race down again; the winning score is based on the combined time for the two runs.

Gretchen Fraser made American skiing history in 1948 when she won the first U.S. gold medal for skiing (by a man or woman) on the slalom course in St. Moritz, Switzerland. Four years later, in Oslo, Andrea Mead Lawrence won the slalom event at the age of 19, despite falling and finishing fourth in her first run. (She also won the 1952 Olympic women's giant slalom title to become the first–and only–U.S. skier to win two gold medals in one Games.) Twenty years elapsed before another American woman—Barbara Ann Cochran—won the slalom gold in 1972, in one of the closest alpine races in Olympic history.

Giant Slalom (GS)

Giant slalom is like the slalom event, although the course is usually longer, a vertical drop of 250–450 meters for men and 250–400 meters for women. Depending on the length of the course, the number of gates will vary, and the gates will be spaced farther apart. The skier still has to make quick, tight turns, however, and do them quickly. The average speed in the GS is 50 mph. There are two runs down the course, and the skier is scored on combined time. When the GS was introduced at the 1952 Games in Oslo, a 19-year-old American, Andrea Mead Lawrence, was the first gold medalist in this event, winning the competition (which at that time required only a single run) by 2.2 seconds.

Mike Powell/ALLSPORT

Hermann Maier of Austria pulls out of a turn during the men's giant slalom event at the 2000 Skiing World Cup Competition in Park City, Utah.

Steve Powell/ALLSPORT

Picabo Street of Team USA trains for the women's downhill event at
the 1994 Winter Olympics in Lillehammer, Norway.

Super G (SG)

This event, a combination of downhill and giant slalom, made
its debut at the 1988 Olympic Winter Games in Calgary, Alberta,

Canada. There is a three-day official training period before the Super G races, giving skiers an opportunity to take a look at the course beforehand. In this popular event, the courses are longer than in the giant slalom, with a vertical drop of 500–650 meters for men and 350–600 meters for women. Speed and passing through gates, which are farther apart than those in the GS, are required for the Super G. The skiers make only one run down the course, which determines their score.

Combined (CO)

At the Olympic Winter Games and World Championships, the combined event consists of two separate races—one downhill and one slalom—usually on shorter courses, with the winner determined by the combined best time. In other competitions, final skier standings in the combined event are usually determined by using the "Lowry Factor," a formula devised by the late Warren Lowry, a former USSA volunteer and FIS Calculations Committee chair. Rather than a total time for the two events (DH, SL), a factoring formula calculates points for each of the two races and determines the overall score and finish for each skier.

Mike Powell/ALLSPORT

U.S. skier Evan Dybvig hits a turn during the moguls qualification event for the World Freestyle Ski Championships in Whistler, British Columbia, Canada.

Freestyle Competitions

The term *freestyle skiing* came from the comparatively "free" skiing style it employed. Early freestyle competitions consisted of one run that featured ballet, moguls, and sometimes aerial moves. Freestyle skiing as it is known today, however, has just two parts: *aerials* and *moguls*. (Ballet was dropped as a competitive event following the 1999–2000 season.) Aerials and moguls require as much skill, strength, and flexibility as a top-notch gymnastics routine. Freestyle skiing was added to the Olympic program in 1992, when competition in moguls was held. Aerial events were added in 1994.

Moguls are bumps, or mounds, under the snow. The moguls slope is 230–270 meters long, with mounds up to 1.2 meters

Nathan Bilow/ALLSPORT

Jonny Moseley of Team USA shows his gold-medal-winning form in the men's moguls at the 1998 Winter Olympic Games in Nagano.

high. The skier must complete two mandatory jumps and midair maneuvers when skiing the moguls event, but can include other jumps of his or her choice. There are two runs over the moguls field, and the judges look for speed, accurate turns, commanding style, and confident movements. Turns should be small and fast and demonstrate control of the skis. They account for 50 percent of the score, with midair maneuvers (twists and jumps) making up 25 percent. The time in which a skier finishes his or her run accounts for the remaining 25 percent of the score. Moguls are only for older, experienced skiers who understand and accept the risks involved.

Nathan Bilow/ALLSPORT

Eric Bergoust of Team USA displays the high-flying style that earned him the gold medal in men's freestyle aerials at Nagano in 1998.

Dual moguls, a head-to-head competition in which the hill is split into two narrower, side-by-side courses (red and blue), is another competitive event in freestyle skiing. Each skier must compete against another skier, completing one run down each of the colored courses. The two scores are added together to determine the winner.

In aerials, skiers perform twists and somersaults—some forward, some backward—after being launched some 50 feet into the air from a ramp (or "kicker"). There may be music playing and an announcer to introduce the skiers. Form makes up 50 percent of the skier's score; the landing is 30 percent, and the takeoff (height and length) accounts for the remaining 20 percent. Aerial skiers practice on trampolines or in the water before ever attempting acrobatic moves on skis.

For safety reasons, there are also age and maneuver limitations in the aerials competition. Double maneuvers may not be performed until a skier is 16 or older, and triple maneuvers may not be attempted until a competitor is 18 or older. No skier may attempt an inverted aerial move (feet above the head) until he or she has been certified by a coach and has completed hours of practice in the pool in the off-season.

5

Nordic Skiing and Ski Jumping

Nordic skiing is skiing across the countryside, not down a steep hill. It's like a fast morning walk, except it's on skis and over snow. Nordic skiing is a great exercise that uses almost every muscle in your body. Nordic skiing also offers skiers more independence, smaller crowds, and no lines at the ski lift. This is the oldest form of skiing. The most common and popular

Brian Bahr/ALLSPORT

Nordic skiers explore the course at Soldier Hollow, the venue for cross-country skiing at the 2002 Winter Olympics in Salt Lake City.

form of Nordic skiing is sometimes referred to as cross-country, "free heel," or "X-C." Some skiers still use the original, "diagonal stride" technique to cross-country ski, although more people are now using the "skating" (or "freestyle") technique, which is faster. In the skating style, skiers will usually keep one ski in the track(s) while pushing off (like a speed skater) with the other ski to gain speed and momentum.

Whatever the preferred name or technique, millions of cross-country skiers enjoy the sport in one form or another every year. It originated in Northern Europe and is becoming more and more popular everywhere, especially with families, who visit ski areas that offer day care and programs designed for children. There are even special sleds available that allow an adult to ski while pulling a toddler along.

Learning Nordic Skiing

Nordic skiing requires equipment and skills that differ from those of alpine skiing. But Nordic skiing is one of the easiest snow sports to learn, and you should be able to master the fundamentals in a beginner's lesson of an hour or less. Alternatively, you can watch more experienced Nordic skiers to learn the basics, even though you will develop your own individual style.

A Nordic practice routine might follow these steps:

- Use any level, snow-covered ground that is handy and accessible—for example, a backyard, playground, or soccer field. Stay away from hard-surfaced roads.

- With skis on, grasp the poles with the pole straps firmly against your hand and next to the thumb.

- With your body weight on the right ski and the left pole, slide the left ski forward. Your right knee should bend and the right heel should lift from that ski.

- Now shift your body weight to the left ski and right pole,

Al Bello/ALLSPORT

Bente Skari of Norway competes in the women's 5-km classic in
the World Cross Country Ski Championships at Salt Lake City.

and slide the right ski forward. Repeat with alternating legs and poles until you are confident about shifting from one ski to the other.

- Pick a point about 100 feet away and, alternating left and right slides, move to your goal. Look ahead, not down at your feet.

Kicking

Once you are comfortable sliding, you will want to learn kicking—that is, pushing off from one ski and gliding on the other. The push-glide motion, or kick, is very familiar to skateboarders and figure skaters. Strong kicks improve distance and are less tiring than trying to slide or shuffle from one spot to the next. Practice kicking using the following sequence:

- With skis together, slide the right ski ahead of the left by a few inches.

- Push off from the left ski and glide on the right. Alternate: Push off from the right ski, glide on the left; left ski push, right ski glide, and so on.

- At first your kicks will be short, but they will get longer and smoother as you get into the rhythm of kicking off and gliding.

Poling

Ski poles add power to Nordic skiing. Follow these suggestions to generate power:

- Place the left ski and the right arm (with the ski pole firmly grasped) forward.

- Shove the right ski pole into the snow up to the basket and even with the left ski.

- Grasp the poles firmly, but not so tightly that wrists and forearms become tense.

- Repeat with the right ski and left arm.

- To double-pole, put both ski poles forward and into the snow. Push off from both poles at the same time. Your arms will extend behind as you move forward. This is a good technique for downhill or uphill slopes.

Nordic Equipment and Clothing

If you only cross-country ski occasionally (four to five times per ski season), renting equipment probably makes the most sense. Ask people at the ski area what type of equipment is best for you. They may be more knowledgeable than salespeople in department or sporting goods stores. A person working in a store that specializes in winter sports equipment, however, should also know what equipment to recommend. Be sure to tell the salesperson how often you ski cross-country, how far you travel on these trips, and where you go. (For more information on Nordic skiing equipment, see Chapter 7, "Equipment and Clothing.")

A Cross-country Ski Trip

Among Americans, alpine was the more popular type of skiing for many years, until resorts became crowded, lift lines grew long, fees went up, and so did the cost of equipment. In the 1960s, interest in health and fitness increased, and thousands of Americans turned to cross-country skiing for the pleasure it gave and the fitness it promoted.

Where to Ski Cross-country

Close to home there may be unused, snow-covered golf courses or farmland where you can ski cross-country. Some sporting goods stores may have brochures or pamphlets available describing ski resorts or Nordic centers in your area. Alternatively, you can check the U.S. Government pages of your telephone book under "Department of the Interior" for information on national parks and national forests. Widen your choices by writing to the Division of Tourism in the capital of the state where you'd like to ski. The agency may have brochures or maps giving information on the state's cross-country ski locations. You'll want specific information on trails: How many are there? What are they like? Are they marked? Are they prepared with tracks? Ski rental costs, trail fees, and charges for lessons are other considerations.

Ski on a trail that is suited for your ability and experience. A beginners' trail is about 1.2–1.8 miles (2–3 km), and an intermediate trail 3.1–6.1 miles (5–10 km). Experienced skiers can handle a long day of 12.4–18.6 miles (20–30 km) or more.

Courtesy and Safety

All cross-country skiers should exhibit common sense and courtesy on the trails:

- Stay in control of your speed and direction. Ski safely. Don't endanger others.

- Ski cross-country in a group. Have a partner and check each other for frostbite or hypothermia.

- When stopped, do not obstruct the trail. Be certain others can see you.

- Posted warnings and signs should be obeyed. Keep off trails that are closed.

- Report all accidents as soon as possible.

On marked trails, signs provide information on directions, conditions, and hazards. Everyone in your group should read and follow the instructions.

Plan your ski trip before you leave home by checking the weather report and getting a trail map. Be sure to ask guides or patrols about trail conditions. Transport your skis in locked, padded cases, with name tags attached. An extra tag on the inside ensures identification in an emergency. Padded sleeves for skis on rooftop racks for vehicles are common. Before heading out onto the ski trails, wash off any mud, snow, ice, or road dirt from your skis and wax them.

The following are some guidelines to help your day go smoothly:

- Check skis, bindings, and poles before you leave home. Look for cracks or other signs of wear on your skis. Tighten all binding pins if needed. Check basket connection to your ski poles.

- With rental equipment, be sure the boots fit and the bindings clamp securely.

- As with any type of exercise, do some stretching before starting out to loosen up your muscles. Also carry and drink water during your workout so you don't get dehydrated.

- On the trail, yield to skiers coming downhill. Be alert; they are moving faster than you are.

- Ski single file on trails and keep to the right.

- It is all right to pass a slower skier and let a faster skier pass you, but you don't have to get out of the track for the faster skier.

- If the trail is busy and you have to stop, get off the track.

- Always stop and help an injured skier. The National Ski Patrol at the ski area should be contacted in an emergency.

- Don't leave trash on the trail; carry the trash out with you.

- Build fires only if the rules allow. Check first to be safe.

Nordic Competitions

At the first Olympic Winter Games in 1924, the skiing competition featured one ski jumping event, two cross-country events, and one Nordic combined event, which included a separate 18-km ski race and jumping competition. All events were for men only.

Norway's entrant in the Nordic combined was Thorleif Haug, who won the 18-km cross-country race easily. His jump wasn't the longest, but his total points pushed him over the top to win the gold in the combined event. He was third in ski jumping.

Fifty years later, Norwegian historian Jakob Vaage discovered an error in the ski jumping scores. Anders Haugen, a naturalized American citizen from Norway, who had jumped for the United States, was actually the bronze medalist, not Haug. At special ceremonies in Oslo in 1974, Haug's daughter presented Haugen with the bronze medal, since her father had died.

Men's Individual Cross-country Events

At the 2002 Olympic Winter Games, the scheduled Nordic events for men include individual cross-country races of 10 km, 15-km pursuit, 30 km, 50 km, and a 4x10-km relay, as well as a new 1.5-km "sprint" event. The 30-km race was introduced in 1956, the same year the Soviet Union sent athletes to participate. They were strong competition for the previously dominant Scandinavians, although Italians were beginning to break into the winner's circle. To date, the only American to have won an Olympic medal in Nordic skiing is Vermont native Bill Koch, who won the silver medal in the men's 30 km in 1976, using the skating technique which he helped popularize.

Al Bello/ALLSPORT

Top male athletes take part in the 30-km event at the
Cross Country Ski World Cup at Soldier Hollow.

Women's Individual Events

The first cross-country events for women began in Oslo at the
1952 Games. Female athletes competed in a 10-km race, with
Finns winning all the medals. Four years later, a women's cross-
country relay was added, the 3x5 km (now 4x5 km). Today,
women also compete in individual cross-country races of 5 km,
10-km pursuit, 15 km, and 30 km. As in the men's competition,
the new 1.5-km "sprint" event has been added to the 2002
women's Olympic program.

Ski Jumping

Ski jumping (also called "ski flying" on the largest hills) is the
most famous and probably most watched of the Nordic events
at the Olympic Winter Games. Only men participate in this

Al Bello/ALLSPORT

Todd Lodwick of Team USA takes off with his skis in the "V" position
in the Nordic combined event at the 1998 Olympic Games in Nagano.

competition, where the athletes soar through the air, traveling
more than the length of a football field, before attempting to
land safely at the base of the hill.

Ski jumpers must be steady, fearless, and in total control of their
skis and bodies. Skiers need to take a scientific approach to their
jumps, carefully considering the angle of their 8-foot-long skis
and how far they should lean forward. They need powerful
muscles for this stressful event, in which a speed of 90 mph is
not unusual. Every move is calculated based on the laws of
aerodynamics, so the skier can ride air currents down to the
finish line. Ski jumpers try to take off with their skis in a "V"
position, which gives them extra lift and can increase distances
from 3–5 meters on the normal (90-m) hill jump and 5–15 meters
on the large (120-m) hill jump.

Judges watch from a tall box-like enclosure just below and to the side of the chute, the long ramp down from the tower. This gives the judges an excellent view of the skier's takeoff, form, and landing.

The skier begins in the tucked, or hunched, position, helmet fastened securely, as he descends the in-run on the ski tower and chute. At takeoff, he straightens his knees and leans his body forward so that he is almost parallel with his skis. There are no poles; his arms stay lined up with the lines of his legs, and he lands in the Telemark position, with knees and hips bent. He cannot touch the ground or his skis with his hands while in the runout (the smooth, snow-covered area at the base), where he slows and stops.

Five judges, stationed on the side of the jumping hill, judge style from takeoff to landing. Timing, balance, form in midair, perfection, and a landing in the Telemark position are rated. Judges deduct up to four points for not landing in the Telemark position and up to 10 points for a fall. Each of the five judges can award from zero to 20 points (in half-point increments) for style. The highest and lowest of the scores are dropped, and the three remaining scores are then added together.

Sixty distance points are earned for landing at the critical point or "K-point" (derived from the German word *kritisch*), where the jumping hill begins to flatten. In individual jumping, the K-point is 120 m from takeoff on the large hill and 90 m from takeoff on the normal hill. When scoring the normal hill event, two points are added for each meter past the critical point, and two points are subtracted for each meter short. When scoring the large hill event, 1.8 points are added for each meter beyond the critical point, and 1.8 points are subtracted for each meter short. In the team large hill event, the K-point is 120 m. The other major point on the hill is known as the P-point, denoted by blue markings on the sides of the landing area, where the pitch of the hill is the steepest.

Craig Jones/ALLSPORT

Adam Malysz of Poland shows the form he used
in winning the large hill (K120) event at the
FIS World Cup Ski Jumping Competition
at Utah Olympic Park in Park City.

Wind is a critical factor in ski jumping, where safety is always a concern. Coaches help monitor the wind for their skiers and use hand signals to indicate if it's safe to jump or if a skier should wait (for more or less wind). Skiers normally have 15 seconds to make their jump after a green light flashes at the end of the takeoff chute or "table."

Nordic Combined

Superb physical fitness is required to compete in this two-part event, which combines ski jumping and cross-country skiing. Strength, technical skill, and endurance are most important.

Formerly, the Nordic combined event always included a small hill (90-m) jump and a 15–km cross-country ski race. The ski jumping competition would usually be held on the first day, followed by a free technique cross-country race over a set course on the second day. The winner of the ski jumping competition would start first on the second day, and other skiers would follow based on their ski jumping scores. The first skier to cross the finish line on the second day would be the winner.

This is still the most common form of Nordic combined competition. More recently, however, some variations have been introduced.

- **Sprint:** Held all in one day. Usually includes a 120- or 90-m jump and a 7.5-km race.

- **Two-man sprint:** Two-member teams each jump (with their total points divided by two for an average). Then each team skis six laps in a tag-team format around a course that is usually about 1.25 km long, to equal a total of 15 km.

- **Team competition:** Similar to the two-man sprint, but with four team members who all jump. Each team member then skis a 5-km leg of a four-man relay on the cross-country course.

- **Mass-starts:** The reverse of the individual, or traditional, Nordic combined event. Competition begins with a mass-start cross-country race, followed by the ski jumping. In the jumping portion of the event, the skiers jump in reverse order of their cross-country finish.

Jed Jacobsohn/ALLSPORT

Jari Mantila is one of Finland's top performers in the Nordic combined event. Here he competes at the 1998 Winter Games in Nagano.

Biathlon

Although the biathlon is a separate Olympic Winter Games sport, it does require elements of Nordic (cross-country) skiing while shooting at targets along the course. This event was introduced to the Olympic program at the 1960 Games. Skiers must shoot from standing and prone (on the ground) positions; penalties are assessed for missing targets. The men's biathlon includes 10-km and 20-km competitions and a 4x7.5-km relay, as well as a 12-km pursuit event that has been added for 2002. Women compete in 7.5- and 15-km races, a 4x7.5-km relay, and a 10-km pursuit event.

6

Snowboarding

As winter sports go, snowboarding is a youngster, just a little more than 35 years old. The first snowboards were little more than sheets of plywood or a pair of skis with a rope tied at the front to hold on to for stability. The high technology developed in ski manufacturing transferred easily and rapidly to snowboards, and today's boards are as complex and technologically advanced as any skis.

Allsport UK/ALLSPORT

Karine Ruby of France won the giant slalom during the 2001 FIS World
Snowboarding Championships at Madonna di Campiglio, Italy.

Learning to Snowboard

Surfers and skateboarders have little difficulty when making the transition to snowboarding. Their skills transfer, and learning the new sport does not take much time. There are few age limits, but you do need to be physically fit and well coordinated to snowboard and enjoy the experience. You control the board by shifting your body weight to the inside or outside edge of the board. If you've surfed or ridden a skateboard, you probably have confidence in your ability to balance on a small, narrow, often wet board.

As with skiing, the easiest and safest way to get started in snowboarding is to take lessons. Learn correctly from the start, and you won't have bad habits you'll need to change later. Lessons are available at some ski resorts as package deals offering snowboarding instruction, board rentals, and lift tickets. There are several magazines devoted entirely to snowboarding, and these are a good information resource. Don't overlook your local parks and recreation department or the U.S. Ski and Snowboard Association. Check the Internet for additional resources.

First Lessons

Try to plan your first snowboarding trip on a day right after a fresh snowfall. Fresh snow is a good cushion and makes snowboarding and falling easier.

Carrying Your Board

Hold your board under one arm, with the bindings against your body and the leash wrapped around your wrist. This gives you control of the board so it won't get away. Alternatively, using both hands, carry the board across your back at the waistline. Be careful not to make any sudden moves that might accidentally hit any other snowboarders or skiers.

Beginning

If you are taking lessons, your practice slope will be gentle, with a good runout at the bottom. Stay away, for now, from the slopes with experienced skiers and snowboarders. Join them when you have some experience and feel confident. Do warmup and stretching exercises: twist, walk, climb, and stretch to get your blood circulating and to increase the oxygen supply to your muscles. (See Chapter 8, "Fitness and Conditioning," for specific recommended exercises.) Check that your board is in good condition, with the bindings and leash secure and the stomp pad in place between the bindings.

Stance

Decide which stance is comfortable and natural for you. First stand sideways on your board with the left foot forward—the regular foot stance. Then stand sideways on your board with the right

Donald Miralle/ALLSPORT

Ricky Bower of Team USA maneuvers above the rim during the men's halfpipe event at the FIS Snowboard World Cup in Park City, Utah.

foot forward—the "goofy" foot stance, a name that originated with surfers. The distance between your feet depends on your snowboarding style, how long your legs are, and, again, what feels comfortable. A stance can be from 14 to 24 inches wide.

Next you'll need to angle your feet, with the front foot turned forward more than the back foot. Bindings adjust independently to get the proper angle for each foot. Start with an average stance width and angles for your style of snowboarding, but feel free to experiment. For example, if you are free-riding on an all-purpose board, and you use a stance width of 20–22 inches, try stance angles of 20° to 30° for the front binding and 5° to 15° for the back. The feel of your board depends on where the bindings are set on the board by the manufacturer. Don't try to move the bindings, except to adjust them for the stance width.

Putting on Your Board

At first, attach your boot only to the front binding.

- Sit down on a flat piece of ground and attach the leash to your front leg to keep the board with you.
- Remove any snow from the binding.
- Step into the binding and secure the ankle strap.
- Secure the toe strap.
- If you have plate bindings with a toe lever, put your front foot in the plate's heel, push your toe down, and flip the toe lever to lock your boot. With a heel lever, reverse the order: toe in first, then lock the heel.

Standing and Centering Your Body

Stand up on your board with the front binding (and leash) attached and get used to the feel and weight of the board. Your foot will point in, which is a strange feeling, but notice that the

Donald Miralle/ALLSPORT

Rosey Fletcher competes for Team USA at the
FIS Snowboard World Cup in Park City.

board is straight. Bending your knees will help you get used to
this stance. Look ahead (not down), and with your back foot
free, use it to push your board on the snow. Try this back and
forth, then side to side. Practice balancing by crouching down
and standing up, using your knees. Alternatively, put all your
weight on the front foot and lift the free foot off the ground.
Now try putting both feet on the board, with the free foot on the
stomp pad. Just stand on the board and get into a comfortable
position.

Control the direction of the snowboard by sliding your hips
forward or backward. This moves your body from the waist
through the end of your spine in a sliding motion, not a bend
from the waist. Practice standing and centering until you are
comfortable with your stance, balance, and the feel of your boots.

Skating

Try skating (or gliding) over the snow instead of walking. Practice this on level ground or on an easy slope:

- Put your weight on the forward foot and push off with the back (free) foot.

- When the board moves, use the stomp pad for your free foot.

- When the board slows, push off again.

- Continue pushing and gliding until you reach your destination.

Edges

Stand on your board with the front foot buckled in and the back (free) foot on the stomp pad. Rock your feet forward onto the toe edge, and your board will dig into the snow. Next, rock your feet backward onto the heel edge, and feel your board dig into the snow. Practice until you can make good, sharp edges in the snow. You'll need them later for stopping, turning, and making ledges in the snow to hold your board.

Walking on the Level and Uphill

On level, snow-covered ground, take short steps, pushing with your free foot and sliding your board along. Take longer steps to move along faster, and keep your board tilted on its forward (tip) edge.

When walking uphill, locate the fall line and place your snowboard across it at a right angle. Put your loose foot on the uphill part of the slope and have the toe edge of your board (with your boot attached) dug in behind you. While lifting and dragging your board, step upward with your free foot. Repeat until you reach the top of the slope. Keep your head up, and always watch for other snowboarders or skiers.

Stopping

The easiest way to stop is just to sit down and skid, but that is very hard on your body and clothes. Here is a better way:

- Turn your board across the fall line.

- Keep your body balanced over the board and your weight even in your boots and bindings.

- Make a hard edge with the uphill side of your board and slow to a stop.

Good Manners

Before starting off, remember that using a few commonsense cautions and good manners will make your day enjoyable and accident free.

- Stay in control of your speed and direction. That applies to your board as well; wear your leash.

- Snowboard safely. Don't endanger yourself or others.

- Snowboard with a friend and check each other for frostbite or hypothermia.

- Yield the right of way and check your blind spot, just as you do when driving a car.

- When stopped, don't be an obstruction to others. Make sure other people can see you.

- Obey posted warnings and signs.

- Keep away from areas that are closed.

- Report all accidents as soon as possible.

- Always stop to help an injured skier or fellow snowboarder. The National Ski Patrol at the ski area should be contacted in an emergency.

- Don't leave any trash behind. Carry the trash out with you.

Snowboarding Competitions

Competitive snowboarding consists of alpine and freestyle events. The alpine events are similar to alpine skiing and have the same goal: get down the course and through the gates as quickly as possible. The two most common races are the slalom and giant slalom, although Super G events are also held. A snowboarder's speed increases relative to the amount of distance between course gates. In slalom, the gates are more tightly placed, as in alpine skiing. In giant slalom and Super G races, the gates are placed farther and farther apart, and snowboarders reach higher speeds.

Before any competition, the snowboarder inspects the course and the gates. The snowboard gates are shorter than alpine skiing gates and are triangle-shaped, so the snowboarders can ride low and tightly around them. Each competitor gets only one run on the course during each round, so he or she needs to be well informed and well prepared.

Snowboarding was a demonstration event at the 1994 Olympic Winter Games and was on the regular program at Nagano in 1998. It is the newest winter sport and is gaining popularity each year. For Salt Lake City, two snowboarding events were scheduled: the giant slalom and the halfpipe. Each event includes separate competitions for women and men.

Nathan Bilow/ALLSPORT

Rosey Fletcher makes a sharp turn around a gate at the
U.S. Snowboard Grand Prix in Mammoth, California.

Shaun Botterill/ALLSPORT

Team USA snowboarder Chris Klug takes a turn in the men's giant slalom
at the 1998 Winter Games in Nagano.

Giant Slalom

Plans for the 2002 Olympics featured a parallel giant slalom
event, run on symmetrical, side-by-side courses with gates. One
course is designated as the red course; the other, the blue course.
Each competitor races one time on each of the two courses. The
snowboarder with the fastest combined score for the two runs
advances to the next round, and the other racer is eliminated.

Halfpipe

This freestyle event takes its name from the shape of the course,
a cylinder cut lengthwise. Snowboarders increase speed on the
sloped portion and then go above the rim of the halfpipe to
demonstrate maneuvers such as jumps and rotations. Winners
are determined by the total number of points received in four
major categories, as scored by five judges:

- Standard maneuvers (without rotation)
- Rotations (spinning tricks)
- Amplitude (average height of maneuvers)
- Overall impression.

The "superpipe"—a longer halfpipe with bigger curved surfaces— was to be featured at the 2002 Olympic Winter Games competition. Using the superpipe shape, snowboarders can perform more difficult and complicated tricks, keep their speed up, and usually land more easily.

Donald Miralle/ALLSPORT

An airborne Ricky Bower of Team USA seems to defy gravity during the men's halfpipe event at the FIS Snowboard World Cup in Park City.

Equipment and Clothing

Hundreds of years ago, two skis worn by the same skier were usually not the same length. One ski was about 10 feet long; the other was shorter and covered with animal skins to make kicking off more efficient. Skis of the same length appeared about 1700. The Telemark model was developed in 1860.

Snowboards have a much shorter history. In 1965, Sherman Poppen, a Michigan man, tied a rope to the front end of a pair of skis he had braced together for his daughters. He called his invention the "Snurfer," combining *snow* and *surfer*. Twelve years later, Jake Burton Carpenter, a New York businessman, moved to southern Vermont and began producing and selling his own version of the Snurfer, and Burton Snowboards were born. Today, snowboards come in many shapes and sizes, and feature various laminates, cores, sidecuts, flex patterns, and colorful graphics.

When considering what equipment to use, a good rule for beginners in any discipline of skiing or snowboarding is: rent first, buy later. Tell people at the ski shop if you're a beginner, intermediate, or expert skier or snowboarder, so you get proper equipment and the right fit. It's not a good idea to buy equipment or clothing when you're young and growing rapidly, because you'll outgrow it too soon. If you do buy equipment and clothing, try the season-ending sales or "swap meets," and take an experienced skier or snowboarder with you to give you advice.

You'll need an assortment of gear: skis and poles or a snowboard, boots, bindings, safety straps, and warm clothes.

Alpine Equipment

About 30 years ago, downhill skis were longer—nearly 7.5 feet in length—and tilted up four inches at the tip, and boot choices were limited. Then, about a decade ago, parabolic (hourglass-shaped) skis were introduced on the market. Although the term parabolic is rarely used now, today's skis still have curves, and technology is more evident than ever. Technological advances in boots have also changed the skiing scene.

Skis

While some skiing veterans still use the longer, straighter skis, the majority of beginners to pro racers are now transitioning to shorter, wider skis. Most industry experts believe that the newer skis can help skiers at all levels improve their technique.

Modern skis are often made in layers of wood and fiberglass on the inside with aluminum on the outside. Metal and titanium alloy laminate skis are also available. Skis with wood cores may last longer but are more expensive. Always ask the experts for their advice.

Many ski shops will allow you to test out, or "demo," skis before you buy them. Ask the technicians or salespeople to help educate you about the different models, brands, and types of technology. Different ski shops carry different ski models, technologies, and designs, so consider renting or testing skis and comparing skis from a few different places before buying. Experiment with different lengths and technologies to see which you prefer before making a purchase.

Skis are measured in three areas: the tip or nose (front), the waist (center area between the tip and tail where the bindings sit), and the tail (back tip). Downhill skis have a center groove for stability and sharp steel edges that cut into the snow. The newer alpine skis are wider at the tips, thicker in the waist, and more curved at the tail. The wider waisted ski, such as an all-mountain ski, gives a skier more stable footing and is a good powder ski. A narrower waisted ski is better on groomed terrain. Skis with wide waists (around 70 mm) and narrower tails (around 85 mm) are good for beginners.

A skier's ideal ski length is determined by several factors: height, weight, skiing ability, and goals for the slopes. Skis are measured in centimeters, and most alpine skis come in lengths of 150-200 centimeters. Beginner to intermediate skiers may want to start on skis that are 4–6 inches shorter than they are. A general guideline for beginners is that, when stood on their tails, the ski tips should reach between the mouth and nose area. Weight is also a factor when recommending ski length and in how the ski works. A heavier person on longer skis can turn with less effort than a lighter person on the same skis. The sales or rental people at the ski shop or your ski instructor can help you decide what ski length is right for you and will ask about your skiing ability.

Type I skiers are considered beginners who ski more slowly and conservatively, and who generally stay on the green or blue (easiest) slopes. Type II skiers prefer a variety of speeds, but still ski moderately, usually on the blue or black trails. Type III skiers are intermediates to experts who ski faster and more aggressively, and who prefer more challenging terrain, such as black diamond or double-black diamond mountain trails.

There are five basic styles of alpine skis:

- **Freeride midfat skis:** These are recommended for skiers who want to enjoy all types of mountain skiing—powder, groomed snow, chopped-up snow, or terrain parks.

- **Freeride fat skis:** These are intended for the skier who enjoys skiing in the deep powder of back bowls.

- **All-mountain skis:** Wider than racing skis, these are best on groomed snow and are recommended for everything except mogul skiing.

- **Expert or racing skis:** Built for speed, these are for the expert or competitive skier.

- **Freestyle skis:** These are primarily for freestyle skiers who plan to jump, twist, and perform tricks in the terrain parks.

Bindings

All ski bindings are designed to release your boot from your ski, which avoids foot, ankle, or leg injuries. Nordic bindings attach at the toe of the boot, while alpine and snowboard bindings grasp both the boot toe and heel. A professional technician, who will use a process called tuning, should set or check all bindings. Bindings should be tight enough to secure the boots to the skis or snowboard, but with enough "give" to detach when you fall, an important safety feature.

Safety Straps or Brakes

Safety straps are another accessory to consider when renting or purchasing skis. A strap from the ski goes around your ankle and buckles or hooks in place. This keeps your skis from barreling down the slope without you and possibly injuring another skier or snowboarder when you fall and the bindings release your skis. Safety straps are recommended for all levels of skiers, unless you want to hike down the mountain to fetch your runaway skis after a fall. Most skis also have built-in brakes. Made from a piece of metal or plastic, the brakes are designed to dig down into the snow automatically when the bindings release the boot.

Boots

Boots control the skis, and the best-fitting boots will provide the best comfort and best skiing. If your feet haven't stopped growing, don't buy boots you can "grow into"; that is guaranteed to make your skiing experience uncomfortable and unpleasant. Ski boots are not walking boots. You'll need other boots with soles designed for walking on snow and ice when you're off the slopes.

To get the proper fit when trying on boots, wear the same type of socks you'll wear when skiing. Bend your ankle forward with the boots unfastened. You should be able to put your index finger in the space between the boot and your leg calf. Fasten the boots. The buckles should be loose enough over the toe for a little "wiggle" room and tighter over the instep. The top should be tight enough to hold the boot against your leg. Your foot should not slip or slide inside the boot, nor should your heel move up and down. Stand on tiptoe. Your toes should not touch the end of the boot or slide forward. Walk around in the boots. They should flex and not pinch anywhere. Boots that hurt in the ski shop will hurt even more on the slopes.

Lined boots will keep your feet warmer, but cost more. Most boot materials are synthetic (man-made) and waterproof, but perspiration can get trapped inside and cause cold, clammy feet. Leather "breathes," but it needs extra care. Wet leather boots should be stuffed with newspaper and left in a warm room to dry, but not close to a heater or fireplace. After they dry, use a waterproofing compound on the boots and re-stuff the toes with newspaper, to keep their shape. Some boots are front entry and others rear, so select the style that works for you. At least one manufacturer has introduced a softer ski boot, with leather wrapping around the boot structure and more cushioning for the feet. This boot is said to provide more flex, as well as easy entry and exit, while still providing support.

Ski Poles

Alpine ski poles should be lightweight and easy to maneuver, with straps that adjust to fit over mittens, gloves, or bare hands. Each pole should have a knob at the top that fits into the crook of your hand, the area between the thumb and forefinger. The strap should fit smoothly along the inside of the hand, so the pole is on top of the strap. At the other end of the pole is a basket made of webbing, with a diameter of 4.5–5 inches. This basket "plants" your ski pole when you are pushing off.

To find the right pole length for your height, turn the pole upside down and grab it above the basket. With your arm bent at the elbow and perpendicular to your body, the end of the pole should be a little higher than your hips. If you can't get an exact fit, go up to the next longer pole, but don't settle for a shorter one. Again, if you are unsure, get help with the sizing from a professional at the ski shop, Nordic center, or ski area.

Nordic Equipment

Skis

Nordic skis are very lightweight, so the skier can stride along easily without becoming tired. Before synthetic materials were available, skis were made of ash, beech, fir, or hickory wood. Today, most Nordic skis are made of fiberglass and put together in layers, with a foam core and a fiberglass top and bottom. Over the fiberglass is plastic, which helps create a durable, maneuverable ski.

All Nordic skis have camber—the upward curve or arch—along the center of the ski bottom. When climbing, a skier's weight on one ski or the other makes the camber flatten and touch the snow. The opposite happens when going downhill: the camber comes off the snow, and the skier moves on the tips and tails. The proper amount of camber gives the beginning skier a lot of flexibility when cross-country skiing.

There are Nordic skis with sidecut (wider at the tip and tail, narrower in the middle), which makes turning easier and provides extra support. If you ski off-track, sidecut skis are a good choice. Parallel-cut skis are the same width all along their length, with no narrowing at the waist. They are used for track skiing (skiing on two deep parallel tracks in the snow).

Get the ski length that's right for you and your height. If your skis are too long, you'll have control problems; if they're too short, they'll dig into the snow. Get shorter skis if you're lightweight for your height, longer skis if you're heavier. Try for good distribution of your weight on the skis.

The five basic styles used for Nordic skiing are:

- **Touring skis:** These are durable and wide, but lightweight (about 6 pounds) and suitable for local parks, woods, and rural areas. They are recommended for the beginning cross-country skier and are the type most commonly available at rental shops.

- **Light touring skis:** Lighter in weight than standard touring skis, these respond faster and can be used on prepared tracks.

- **Racing skis:** These are the fastest and lightest of all, weighing 2.5–3 pounds. They are built from synthetic materials, have parallel cut, and are narrower than touring or mountaineering skis. Some racing skis are boat-cut, with the middle section of the ski wider than the tips and tails. One drawback with racing skis is that they cost about twice as much as standard touring skis.

- **Mountaineering skis:** These are for travel in the wilderness and are lightweight, strong, and durable. They have metal edges that prevent ice and snow damage and are sidecut for easy turns in unmarked areas. Mountaineering skis are for the expert skier, not the beginner.

- **Skate skis:** These are the newest skis available. Instead of skiing in prepared tracks or on untracked snow, which is only for the experienced skier, skate skiers use the stroke of an ice skater to move along.

All Nordic skis have textured ski bottoms that grip the snow when you climb or walk forward, with your weight on one ski; the textured bottoms don't grip when your weight is evenly balanced between the two skis. Which textured pattern you choose depends on temperature and snow conditions.

Ski Poles

Nordic ski poles are made of fiberglass and have curved tips. Like alpine poles, most have adjustable pole straps to fit over the hands, and a knob at the top that fits the crook of the skier's hand, between the thumb and forefinger. Fitting for Nordic ski pole length is similar to alpine poles.

Boots

Nordic ski boots are lightweight and low cut, and they have three holes in the sole where the bindings attach. When trying boots on for the first time (whether renting or buying), wear the same type of socks you'll wear when skiing. (For proper fitting instructions, see the previous section on alpine boots.)

Bindings

For Nordic skiing, the bindings are a sole plate with three pegs that fit into three matching holes in the sole of the ski boot. These clamp into place, using the tip of a ski pole or a thumb. The connection should be tight, so the boot doesn't slip. The foot is anchored only at the front of the boot, leaving the heel free (another name for Nordic skiing is "free-heeling").

Snowboarding Equipment

Try snowboarding a few times using rented equipment before investing in your own board, boots, and bindings. Think about your goals and what you want to be able to do with your snowboard. As with skis, don't be afraid to try before you buy, and take advantage of "demo" programs at ski shops. Try boards made by different manufacturers that feature different technologies. Experiment with boards of different lengths, widths, and stiffness.

Snowboards

A snowboard looks like one short, fat alpine ski and is described with some of the same vocabulary: tip, tail, edge, binding, camber, and base. Unlike an alpine ski, however, a snowboard has a stomp pad, a rectangular nonskid pad between the bindings. Your back foot rests on this pad when it is not in the back binding. Use this pad when getting off a chairlift, for example, to keep you and your board together. Snowboards also have shovels and kicks at both ends. The kick (or rise) lifts your board to the top of the snow. The shovel is the upward curve of the board.

Boards are made with a wood or foam core, although some are aluminum inside. There are layers of other materials on top, and boards vary in weight and softness, as well as width. The flexibility will be soft or hard. Stiff or hard boards are usually longer and best suited for racers and heavier people. Softer boards are usually for freestyle snowboarders and for lighter-weight riders. Longer boards require more energy to use, while shorter boards are easier to maneuver and are better suited to resort terrain parks. Some boards are made specifically for women and children.

The type of board you use depends on your height and weight and the style of snowboarding you choose: freestyle, free riding, or alpine/racing.

- **Freestyle boards** are used on powdery snow for halfpipes, slope style, or for moguls and other jumps. Halfpipe boards are very flexible and hold an edge well. They require soft boots and bindings that are suitable for jumps and tricks (like flips) and have little tail or tip kick.

- **Slope style boards** are like skateboards—wide, flat, and soft. They are needed when doing tricky maneuvers on the snow.

- **Racing and alpine boards** are the strongest boards. Built to withstand high speeds and steep downhill slopes, these are best suited for racers and others who like going fast. Racing boards are stiffer and firmer, with hard bindings and boots like those used with skis. They have very little tail kick, which increases speed. However, there is no release from the board in a fall. Both styles are narrow, but the alpine is a little tougher, for snowboarding in mountains.

- **Free riding boards** are all-purpose boards and the most popular and versatile. Good for snowboarding either freestyle or alpine/racing, they are a good choice for the beginner.

Again, when first trying out a snowboard, ask for help and advice from a ski shop technician or snowboard instructor concerning the length and type of snowboard you should use. As riders become more advanced, they will want to move up to high-end, high-performance boards. Boarders who ski backcountry and carry backpacks may also want to consider a longer board to account for the extra weight of the pack.

Leash

Every snowboard has a leash that attaches your front leg to the front binding. This leash keeps your board from riding away by itself and causing serious problems for others on the slope. A leash is required equipment at all snowboarding areas.

Boots

Snowboarding and ski boots have the same functions: to fit your feet in your bindings, keep your feet dry and warm, and support your feet and ankles. Snowboarding boots come in hard and soft styles.

Soft boots, with high-back bindings, have an inner, thickly padded "bladder" to keep feet warm and dry. The outer part of the boot is made of a soft, flexible material, so the ankle moves easily. The soles have deep treads to grasp the base of the bindings. Hard boots are thick on the inside and have a plastic outer boot, or shell. Their stiff soles clamp into plate bindings.

Racers and alpine riders seem to prefer hard boots with plate bindings, while freestylers, in general, wear soft boots with high-back bindings. A snowboarding boot that is becoming more popular is the hybrid. Hybrid boots are soft, but have hard soles, use high-back bindings, and provide a solid, closer feel between the rider and snowboard.

When trying on boots, wear the same type of socks you'll wear while snowboarding. The fit should be a bit snug because the insides of the boots will compress after the boots have been worn a few times. Your heels should fit well down into the boots and not lift out, but stay in place.

Bindings

Get advice from a professional or an experienced snowboarder when selecting bindings. Your choice of bindings depends on the style of snowboard and kind of snowboarding you do. The bindings must grasp your boots securely but have a dependable release. Step-in bindings are the easiest to use because you don't have to sit in the snow to get on your board.

With soft boots, use bindings with buckled straps and high backs. The backs can be different heights, from tall and stiff to short and flexible, depending on your style. With hard boots, use plate bindings. These lock your boots to the snowboard and support your ankles and lower legs. Plate bindings look like a mousetrap with two traps, one to lock over the toes and one that locks the heel in place. They provide excellent control. Eventually, you may want to customize your bindings by adjusting their straps and/or high backs.

Caring for Your Equipment

Before skiing or snowboarding for the first time each season, it is wise to get a tune-up for your equipment *before* hitting the slopes. Have a pro check the bindings and make any needed adjustments. Before every snowboarding trip, check equipment for cracks, wear, or loose connections.

Ski Maintenance

If your skis show signs of wear—fiberglass layers separating, binding screws loose, or deep nicks and gouges—you can do simple repairs using ordinary tools like a screwdriver, putty knife, and waxed paper. Ski repair kits containing all the materials (and step-by-step instructions) needed to do simple repairs are on the market for do-it-yourselfers.

Unexpected moisture is a ski's worst enemy. Never leave wet, snow-covered skis standing on their tails in a warm room. The tails will soak up water from melted snow and, the next time out on the slopes, the water will freeze and the tails will crack.

When transporting skis on a plane or other commercial transportation, rent, borrow, or buy a padded case with locks to protect them. Rooftop ski racks are available when traveling by motor vehicle, but protect your bindings from the elements during transport if possible. Be sure to wash off all road dirt, mud, salt, ice, and snow before waxing your skis and/or schussing down a slope.

At the end of the season, lubricate the bindings and wax the ski bottoms before storing. Leave skis in a dry, cool room in a vertical position with their tails down until your next skiing season. To preserve the camber of wood skis, tape them with their bottoms together and insert a piece of wood in between.

Waxing

A good glide wax on skis provides a smooth ride downhill (or on level ground) and the speed to "run" on the snow. The wax you select must suit snow conditions, daytime temperatures, and humidity. The general rule is to use hard wax for dry snow when the temperature is below 25°F (–4°C). Use soft wax for wet snow when the temperature is above 35°F (2°C). Check the snow by picking up a handful (wearing gloves!) and squeezing it. Wet snow will form a ball and roll easily along the ground; dry snow won't.

Wax your skis indoors in a warm room and be sure they are dry and clean of all dirt. Otherwise, the wax won't stick.

- Use a smooth wax for cold, powdery snow.

- If the temperature is above 32°F (0°C), use a topcoat over the base coat.

- Apply the base coat and rub it in with a cork. Repeat as needed.

- Test the wax job by skiing. If there is not enough wax, the skis will slip going uphill.

- If there is too much wax, the skis will have too much grip, and you will have to push harder with your ski poles. In that case, some wax may have to be scraped off.

If the temperature changes during the day and the weather gets warmer, for example, you may need to re-wax or use a different wax. If the snow gets heavy and slushy, use klister wax, which is very sticky and hard to use, and takes time to dry.

Snowboard Maintenance

The best maintenance for snowboards (or skis) is preventive. Carry your board in a locked, padded bag whenever you travel, or use a locking roof rack on top of a car. These precautions will save your board from unexpected nicks, dents, and needless repairs. With a few basic tools, you can learn to file and bevel edges and to clean, repair, and wax the base. Repair kits for do-it-yourselfers are on the market; however, some repairs need an expert's touch. If parts of your board separate—a process called *delaminating*—or if there are deep gouges that have to be filled in, you'll want the repairs done by a professional.

Wax

After snowboarding two or three times, you'll want to wax your board to keep it in top shape for gliding and turning. Start with a clean base, removing all dirt, grime, or salt buildup. If you don't want to give your board a hot wax, carry a bar of soap and use it as a substitute. Soap wears off, however, and needs to be reapplied regularly. There are spray waxes available which are convenient to carry and handy to use on the slopes.

Clothing

Before investing in ski or snowboard attire, decide if you will use these clothes for other activities. Do you want an all-purpose jacket that you can also wear for backpacking or biking? Will the jacket be easy to stow when you remove it? How much do you want to spend? Layering is an important concept that, if done correctly, will keep you warm and dry whether you are skiing, snowboarding, or participating in some other outdoor activity. A store that specializes in skiwear will be able to give you sound advice. Always try on your ski clothes at the store.

Jackets and Parkas

An insulated jacket (waist length) or a parka (hip length) should not be too heavy, and should breathe, allowing moisture from your body to escape. It should protect you from the elements—wind, rain, or snow—and may be waterproof. Look for air vents that can be opened or closed when you want either to seal warmth in (and keep cold out) or to cool off. Some newer ski parkas and jackets have ultra-thin, but effective, insulation, which reduces bulk. One of the latest innovations is a battery-powered fleece jacket with heat-technology panels that are laminated to the fleece, which is supposed to maintain the perfect heat level for your body.

Outerwear should be roomy enough to allow you to wear at least two other layers—the base and middle layers. The base layer should be a fabric such as a polypropylene shirt or turtleneck that wicks moisture away from your body. The middle layer should help keep you warm by trapping air, but not moisture, insulating your body from the cold. This could be a fleece sweater, but should be something that breathes and dries quickly. Avoid cotton because it can absorb up to 200 percent of its weight in water and will hold moisture close to your skin. As your body heats up, a layer can be removed and stored. You'll reverse the process later in the day, putting clothes back on as your body cools when the temperature drops.

Head Gear

Up to 55 percent of body heat can escape through an uncovered head, so wear a hat that also covers your ears. One-piece hoods that cover the face and neck, with openings for the nose and eyes, are also an option. Some skiers wear baseball caps with vented tops in warm weather; the visor gives extra eye protection. Consider wearing a fleece gaiter or scarf to keep your neck warm, especially on the high-speed chair lifts. More skiers are now wearing helmets, which provide warmth and head protection.

Some skiers report that they feel more confident in a helmet, and that may improve performance on the slopes. As always with ski gear, fit is the important consideration.

Mittens and Gloves

Mittens are warmer, but gloves give a better grip on ski poles. Make sure the mittens or gloves are warm and waterproof, to keep your hands dry. Many snowboarders are now using modified mittens with a free forefinger, which allows more dexterity and still keeps hands warmer than typical gloves. Use thermal glove liners to keep the warmth inside.

Socks

Wear two pairs of socks, a polypropylene pair underneath and a wool pair on top; the first pair wicks the moisture away from your feet, while the second pair keeps your feet warm. Look for socks of different lengths and thermal styles in sporting goods stores or ski shops.

Ski or Snow Pants

Waterproof ski or snow pants can be worn over sweatpants or thermal underwear. Some skiers and snowboarders like to wear jeans or baggy pants, but denim or cotton pants will take longer to dry if they get wet. Many skiers prefer bib overalls, as they keep the wind out and eliminate air gaps at the waist when worn under a parka or jacket. Snowboarders should look for reinforced areas at the knees and seat, since riders spend a lot of time kneeling and sitting down to rest or adjust equipment.

For Cross-country Skiing

Wear clothes that are comfortable and roomy, since your body needs to move easily. Use the layering system, with clothes that are lightweight but warm. Remember to wear a hat and warm gloves or mittens. Wear thermal underwear made from a fiber that holds warmth next to your body, but which breathes (e.g., silk, polypropylene, a wool blend, etc). Any shirts should be long enough to tuck inside your ski pants. Knickers are popular with some cross-country skiers. They should be snug around the calf, but not too tight in the legs. Denim pants are not recommended for cross-country skiing because they won't keep you warm and won't dry out easily if they get wet.

As with alpine skiing or snowboarding, wear warm but breathable socks that will wick away moisture from your feet. Be sure the socks are long enough. For skiing through deep snow, you might also want to wear gaiters (leggings) that keep the snow out of your boots.

If you are going on an all-day trip, you will have to pack supplies: snacks, water, ski wax, spare parts. Daypacks are large and can be heavy, but are needed for extended cross-country skiing. (Waist or fanny packs are ideal for shorter jaunts.) A pack should be narrow enough so that your arms don't hit it while using your ski poles. Wide shoulder straps keep the pack from slipping and distribute its weight more efficiently.

8

Fitness and Conditioning

If you run, bike, or ride a surfboard or skateboard, skiing is almost perfect as a cross-training sport. You may be fit already, but there are exercises you can do to make yourself even more fit for the rigors of Nordic or alpine skiing or snowboarding. Whether you are a recreational or competitive skier or snowboarder, there are always benefits to keeping your body in top physical condition.

Physical Fitness

It's never too soon, or too late, to begin exercising and getting your body physically fit. If you are flabby, get winded easily, are overweight, or are otherwise out of shape, you may have trouble skiing, snowboarding, or taking part in any strenuous exercise. You should consult with your physician, however, before beginning any new workout program.

The Four Parts of Fitness

Physical fitness has four parts: *muscle strength, muscle endurance, cardiovascular endurance* (heart, lungs, and blood vessels), and *flexibility*. Each part depends on the others to maintain physical fitness.

Resistance training, for example, builds strength into muscles by working with resistance that represents 60 percent or more of a one-repetition maximum. Muscle endurance is built by working muscles over a period of time without tiring them. Any exercises involving a high number of repetitions (20 or more) are great ways to create high-endurance muscle. Muscles need oxygen to function at peak levels. This is why the heart, lungs, and blood vessels are so important to physical fitness. They sustain working muscles over long periods of time during practices and competitions.

Muscle Strength

Muscle strength can prevent aches and pains; keep your body aligned properly, and protect against injuries. Building muscle strength requires the skier to exercise more intensely than with any other type of physical training. Exercising with heavy resistance loads—while keeping the time that the muscle is under tension below 20 seconds—produces the best strength gains. During exercise, the muscles should feel uncomfortable, but not painful. Remember: Your goal is *overall* muscle strength, since too much strength in one group of muscles can lead to injury in another group.

Some suggested muscle-strength exercises include:

- *Abdominal curls*—for a strong abdomen and lower back.

- *Squats* (not a full squat)—for strong hips, lower back, buttocks, thighs, calves, and ankles.

- *Military presses*—for strong shoulders and postural muscles.

- *Pull-ups*—for the back, biceps and forearms.

- *Dips*—for upper body musculature, including chest and triceps.

Muscles need recovery and muscle-building time, so take a day off in between workouts.

Muscle Endurance

Muscle endurance exercises build stamina and help the body to perform at its best during a competition. Vigorous exercises such as jogging, bicycling, and swimming are excellent for achieving muscle endurance. They also increase heart and lung efficiency and improve an athlete's overall personal appearance.

Cardiovascular Endurance

Many doctors regard skiing as a superb cardiovascular fitness exercise. As a low-stress outdoor activity, it is excellent for seniors, who make up 13 percent of skiers. Cardiovascular endurance is achieved through exercises performed for at least 20 minutes. Walking, jogging, running, bicycling, swimming, dancing, and skipping rope are other activities that raise the heart rate, take oxygen into the body, and move it to the muscles, which then provide the energy for the exercise you are doing.

Unfavorable weather and unhealthy air sometime interfere with outdoor endurance exercises, so gyms have become more popular with athletes. However, several endurance exercises can be done at home even in a small space. When exercising on a rug, wear gym socks; on a hard floor, shoes that cushion your feet are best. Stationary bicycles are widely available and can be ridden to fit your schedule, regardless of the weather. Other indoor endurance exercises include jogging in place, jumping jacks, jumping rope, and doing side hops. Bowling regularly is a good indoor exercise for building muscles in the shoulders, forearms, lower back, and legs, and can supplement a fitness program at the gym.

Flexibility

Flexibility exercises—for example, bends, stretches, swings, twists, lifts, and raisers—can be used to stretch out muscles that have "tightened" from vigorous exercise, as in a competition. Do flexibility exercises to warm up and start the adrenaline rush that will help propel you downhill or cross-country.

Motor Fitness

Motor fitness includes coordination, speed, balance, and agility. Body muscles and body senses, especially the eyes, build coordination. Repeating certain eye and body movements—for example, catching a ball—builds coordination. Speed is built through brief exercises that demand lots of energy and effort. Short sprints are excellent speed builders.

Preparation

Although exercising regularly year-round is preferable, beginning an exercise program a month or even six weeks before a skiing or snowboarding trip will prepare the body for the rigors of the expedition. Exercise improves circulation, lubricates your joints, increases oxygen and blood flow, and helps reduce injuries. Beginners, especially, need regular exercise.

Start with a few repetitions and then increase the number each day. Drink water to keep from getting dehydrated and to prevent your muscles from cramping.

Limber Up

Limber up by doing these exercises for half an hour every day:

- Stand with your knees and feet together.
- Reach up with both hands as high as you can, keeping your feet on the floor. Hold for a count of 10.
- Slowly lower hands.
- Repeat three to four times.
- Stretch out your arms with the palms up and swing them back.
- Hold that position and relax, keeping your arms outstretched. Then, push back a little more.

- Stretch out your arms with the palms up and bend your body at the knees. Keep your feet on the floor, your knees together, and your upper body straight.

- Try this five times at first, then increase.

- Repeat the knee bends, but stand on your toes, not with your feet flat on the floor.

Modify your daily routine by biking, walking up stairs, running, or swimming. Jumping rope can be done inside and is great for balance and coordination. Try jumping, at first, for one to two minutes, but jump with both feet at once and try to do more and more jumps per minute rather than jumping for a longer time. This prepares you for those short spurts of energy needed when skiing or snowboarding. Do leg lifts, leg raises, jumps, and twists to strengthen muscles and build endurance. Squeezing a hard rubber handball strengthens wrists and hands, and keeps fingers flexible.

9

Health and Nutrition

To succeed in any sport, an athlete needs to maintain good health for peak performance. Unhealthy athletes injure easily and seldom win medals for themselves or their team.

Nutrition

Good eating habits go hand-in-hand with fitness training. An athlete can't become physically fit without eating a well-balanced diet. One of the best ways to ensure that you are in top form is to follow the recommendations of the Food Guide Pyramid, introduced by the U.S. Department of Agriculture (USDA) and the U.S. Department of Health and Human Services in 1992. By eating the recommended groups of foods in the suggested amounts, you are giving your body the nutrients—including carbohydrates, protein, fat, vitamins, and minerals—it needs to perform at its peak.

The dietary guidelines of the Food Guide Pyramid, the basis of federal nutrition policy, are easy to follow:

- Eat a variety of foods.
- Balance the food you eat with physical activity.

- Choose a diet with plenty of grains, vegetables, and fruits.

- Choose a diet low in fat (especially saturated fat) and cholesterol.

- Choose a diet moderate in sugars and salt.

Eating a properly balanced diet of nutritious foods is part of being an athlete. Many athletes may actually need more than the suggested daily servings or calories to provide the power and strength they need to train and compete. Several factors influence the amount of energy that an athlete needs. These include the type, intensity, and frequency of training, as well as the size, age, and sex of the athlete. For example, athletes who engage in short-burst, high-intensity events will have different energy needs from those who engage in sports that require longer endurance.

A Guide to Daily Food Choices

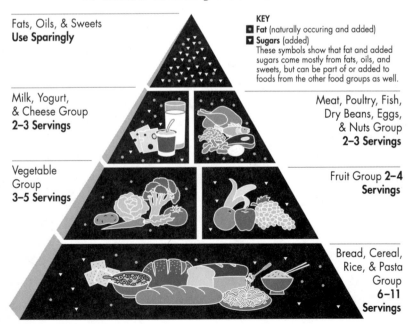

Source: U.S. Department of Agriculture and
U.S. Department of Health and Human Services

Foods for Peak Performance

Foods that are ideal for peak performance contain carbohydrates and fat for energy (to fuel the body) and protein (for growth, maintenance, and repair of body tissues). Carbohydrates are the body's main source of energy. They should make up between 55 and 65 percent of your daily intake of calories. There are two types of carbohydrates: simple and complex.

Simple carbohydrates, also called simple sugars, are found in sweet and sticky foods such as candy, soft drinks, and sweet desserts. You should avoid simple carbohydrates, since these are "empty calories," meaning they may taste good, but they do not provide the body with nutrition. It is not necessary to eliminate them entirely from your diet, but be selective. Sugar in its natural form is abundant in fresh fruit. To satisfy a sweet tooth, it's better to eat a piece of fruit than a candy bar.

Complex carbohydrates that come from plants are called starches and should make up the majority of carbohydrate fuel. Complex carbohydrates consist of hundreds of simple sugars linked together. In your digestive tract, complex carbohydrates are turned into glucose (a simple sugar) by enzymes. Your body absorbs this simple sugar and turns it into energy. Complex carbohydrates are found in breads, cereals, pasta, starchy vegetables such as corn and potatoes, dried beans and peas, and fruits. Vitamins and minerals are abundant in many of these foods.

Protein is found in several kinds of foods. We get animal protein from dairy products (for example, milk and cheese), eggs, meats, poultry, and fish. Be sure to choose lean meats and low-fat dairy products. Protein is also found in grains, nuts, legumes, and seeds. Try to keep your protein consumption to about 10–15 percent of what you eat each day, and you'll consume enough to build muscle, maintain it, and repair it when necessary.

Next to water, your body is made up primarily of protein. Protein provides the building blocks for your body to grow and to replace or repair damaged cells. Each protein molecule is made up of 20 amino acids. Your body makes only 11, so you need to get the other nine—called essential amino acids—from the foods you eat. Because your body can't store protein, you need to eat protein every day.

Like carbohydrates, fat is an important fuel source, but fat has twice as many calories as an equal weight of carbohydrates. A little goes a long way to keep an athlete healthy and fit. A diet that is moderately low in fat will not hinder performance. The fat you eat should come from vegetable oils or nuts and should constitute no more that 30 percent of total calories consumed.

Healthy snacking will help keep you in top form. For the skier or snowboarder who is serious about getting and staying fit, there is no place for high-fat, high-salt, or high-calorie "junk food" in the diet. Try eating apples, oranges, or carrot and celery sticks when you need or crave a snack during the day. Don't let yourself get hungry when you're out in the cold.

Eating regular meals is also important. Don't skip meals— especially breakfast, which is the most important meal of the day. Breakfast is like putting gas in a car—you need it to get started. It should include a protein source, a bread or cereal, a fruit or vegetable, and a small amount of fat and milk. It should be a solid one-third of your daily calorie intake.

Not hungry for breakfast in the morning? Try eating a light dinner the night before. You'll have an appetite in the morning, and that should help to get you on a regular meal schedule. If you don't find the "traditional" breakfast interesting, there is nothing wrong with eating a baked potato, having a hearty soup, or eating lean meat, fish, or poultry at your first meal of the day. The important point to learn is to eat well-balanced, nutritious meals throughout the day, starting with the first one.

Weight Management

Weight should be managed through a proper program of nutrition. Follow the advice of a family physician, health care professional, or sports nutritionist regarding the diet and fitness training program that is best for you.

There are no "miracle" foods, diets, or pills that will keep you in perfect health and physically fit. A well-balanced diet, paired with regular exercise, will help you to stay in good shape for life.

Water and Fluid Replacement

Food isn't the only key to peak performance. Water is just as important. Of all nutritional concerns for athletes, proper hydration is most critical. One of the key functions of fluids is body temperature control. Dehydration can hinder performance and lead to serious medical complications.

Water makes up 60 percent of your body's weight. It is the one nutrient you need the most of every day. All your organs depend on water to function. Water helps in digestion and carries other nutrients and oxygen to all your cells. It is needed to lubricate your joints and to maintain body temperature. One to two quarts of water each day will keep your body well lubricated and prevent dehydration.

The main point to remember about staying hydrated is to drink regardless of whether you feel thirsty. Thirst is a sign that your body has already started to dehydrate. Dehydration is a condition that occurs when the body loses more fluids than it takes in. Drink before, during, and after skiing, snowboarding, or other exercise, whether you are competing or just working out. The best beverage choice is water, the simplest fluid for your body to absorb.

Sports drinks and diluted juices (one part juice, one part water) provide another good choice for fluid replacement. Extremely concentrated beverages like sodas or undiluted fruit drinks and juices are not useful for immediate fluid replacement and could give you a stomachache while you are training or competing. Cola drinks, coffee, and tea are loaded with caffeine and act as diuretics, actually dehydrating you more.

When training or competing, the suggested amounts you should drink are as follows:

- 2 cups cool water about two hours before training or competition.

- 1 to 2 cups water 15 minutes before training or competition.

- 4 to 6 ounces water every 15 minutes during training.

- 2 cups water for every pound of weight loss after competition or training.

Health Hazards

Cigarettes

It is estimated that 4.5 million young Americans between the ages of 11 and 17 are cigarette smokers. The use of tobacco is addictive. Cigarette smoking during adolescence leads to significant health problems, including respiratory illnesses, decreased physical fitness, and retardation in lung growth and function. Smoking is not recommended for anyone, and those who do smoke will find that they have less lung capacity when exercising.

Illegal Drugs

The message all athletes and Americans need to hear is that drug usage is illegal, dangerous, unhealthy, and wrong. Marijuana is the most widely used illicit drug in the United States and tends to be the first illegal drug teens use.

Marijuana smoking is dangerous. It is not a "safe" alternative to alcohol or tobacco. Marijuana blocks the messages going to the brain and alters one's perceptions, emotions, vision, hearing, and coordination. Marijuana has six times as many carcinogens (cancer-causing agents) as tobacco, and today's marijuana is much more potent, creates dependency faster, and often becomes an "entrance" drug—one that can lead to dependence on "hard" drugs like cocaine.

Thirty years of research have pinpointed the effects of smoking marijuana. According to Monika Guttman, who writes extensively about drug use, "Marijuana reduces coordination; slows reflexes; interferes with the ability to measure distance, speed and time; and disrupts concentration and short-term memory." Each of these effects would be detrimental to any athlete, especially a skier or snowboarder.

Steroids

Many athletes—even Olympic athletes—have used drugs of some type for many years. Such drugs are sometimes called "performance-enhancing," but, in reality, they are not. Steroids, amphetamines, human growth hormone (hGH), and erythropoietin (EPO) are a few drugs specifically banned by the International Olympic Committee (IOC). An athlete's misuse of drugs threatens not only the health of that athlete, but also the dignity of the sport. Unfortunately, drug education alone has not been a sufficient deterrent to drug abuse, and sport authorities have also had to employ the threat of public disclosure and punitive action if an athlete fails a drug test.

The American Medical Association (AMA), U.S. Anti-Doping Agency (USADA), World Anti-Doping Agency (WADA), and National Collegiate Athletic Association (NCAA) have deplored the use of steroids for muscle building or improved athletic performance. Steroids (anabolic-androgenic steroids, or AAS) are a drug danger, with terrible consequences for the user.

The food additive androstenedione, or "andro," has been identified as a steroid. The USADA, WADA, and NCAA, as well as other sports organizations, have banned its use by athletes.

Steroid abuse is an increasing problem among teenagers. Steroid use by males can result in breast development, hair loss, and acne, plus yellowish skin and eyes. Among females, breasts shrink, hair grows on the face and body, and menstrual cycles can become irregular. For both males and females, the result of steroid use can be a permanent stunting of bone growth and permanent damage to the heart, liver, and kidneys. Steroid abuse also raises the risk of strokes and blood clots.

The psychological effects of steroid use are just as devastating, according to the American Sports Education Institute, which has noted the following: "Wide mood swings ranging from periods of violent, even homicidal, episodes known as 'roid rages' to depression, paranoid jealousy, extreme irritability, delusions, and impaired judgment."

Effects of using EPO can range from sterility to increased risk of heart attack, liver and kidney disease, and some cancers. EPO and amphetamines have caused deaths in athletes, and the long-term affects on a normal-size person of using human growth hormone are still unknown.

In addition to steroids, the World and U.S. Anti-Doping agencies prohibit hundreds of substances that claim to enhance athletic performance. For more information on banned substances, contact either the:

World Anti-Doping Agency (WADA)

Internet: http://www.wada-ama.org/

or

United States Anti-Doping Agency (USADA)

1265 Lake Plaza Drive

Colorado Springs, CO 80906

Tel: (719) 785-2000

Fax: (719) 785-2001

Internet: http://www.usantidoping.org/

Drug reference line: (800) 233-0393

Drug prevention materials for young people and adults are available by contacting the USADA.

Vision Care

If you wear corrective lenses and are a budding or serious skier or snowboarder, ask your eye doctor if contact lenses would be suitable for you. Today's contacts come in hard and soft materials and are lightweight; some can be worn for hours at a time. In fact, there are disposable contact lenses that can be worn 24 hours a day, don't need special cleaning, and can be disposed of after seven days. Disposable lenses are fairly expensive, however, and may not be suitable for a young, growing athlete. Always check with your doctor and get the benefit of a professional recommendation for your unique needs.

If you wear the traditional contacts, be sure to have your cleaning and wetting solutions with you when you practice and compete, and let your coach know you wear contacts.

10

Safety and First Aid

Safety precautions are as necessary in skiing and snowboarding as they are in any other sport. Although snow is an excellent cushion for spills, skiers and snowboarders need to be aware of the dangers of frostbite, hypothermia, and other climate- and weather-related problems before heading out to the slopes.

Recreational skiing and snowboarding are relatively safe sports, but bumps and bruises do happen. Learning a few safety rules, including the following, can help prevent serious injuries:

- Wear the right clothes. Layering clothing can help keep you warm and dry. Don't forget hats, scarves, neck gaiters, and/ or gloves.

- Go through a warmup session and do stretching exercises before skiing or snowboarding. This will help prevent muscle strains and other aches and pains.

- If you're not feeling well, don't ski or snowboard. You'll make a quicker recovery and be in better shape than if you skied or went snowboarding while "under the weather."

- Drink plenty of water. Dehydration can happen quickly, so don't wait until you're thirsty to get a drink. You can choose a sports drink, but water tastes just as good and is usually free. Consider carrying a refillable water bottle.

First Aid Kit

All sports include the risk of injury. Therefore, it's wise to know what to do to handle those inevitable bumps, bruises, scrapes, or more serious injuries.

Keeping a well-stocked first aid kit is essential. The American Red Cross recommends carrying a small first-aid kit and/or keeping a winter supply kit in your vehicle for emergencies. If you are at an established ski area, you should seek professional help from the National Ski Patrol or a resort employee as soon as possible. If you are skiing in the backwoods, off trail, or anywhere else where professional assistance may not be immediately available, having the following items with you could help in case of an emergency, until you can get the injured person to a medical center:

- Sterile adhesive bandages in different sizes
- Safety pins in assorted sizes
- Soap
- Latex or vinyl gloves
- Sunscreen
- Gauze pads
- Triangular bandages
- Pain relievers and other drugs (e.g., antacids, anti-diarrhea medicine, syrup of ipecac to induce vomiting, activated charcoal, antibacterial ointment)
- Ace bandages for ankles, knees, and ribs
- Roller bandages
- Butterfly bandages or Steri-Strips®

- Adhesive tape
- Scissors
- Tweezers
- Needle
- Sterile towelettes or antiseptic wipes
- Thermometer
- Tongue depressors
- Petroleum jelly or other lubricant
- Instant cold packs
- Sugar packets or glucose tabs
- Salt packets
- Antihistamine and decongestants
- Rehydration packets
- Ammonia caps or smelling salts for dizziness
- Cardboard arm and leg (box) splints
- First aid instruction book, including CPR instructions
- Bulb syringes
- "Zip-lock" baggies
- Blanket
- Penlight/flashlight

Have a list of emergency telephone numbers taped inside the first aid kit, but in a real emergency, you can dial 911. Be sure you know where there's a telephone (most Ski Patrol members now carry mobile phones), and keep some spare change in the first aid kit in case you need to use a pay phone. At competitions, a physician, nurse, or other trained health care professional should be available to take care of serious injuries should they occur.

These guidelines may also be helpful:

- Always remain calm. Don't panic or appear flustered. Others around you will take their behavioral cues from you.

- Don't try to be a doctor. When in doubt about the severity of any injury, get the skier or snowboarder to a doctor or let the doctor, nurse, or health care professional on duty make the decision.

- *Never* move a skier or snowboarder who may have a serious injury. This can make matters worse. Be safe, not sorry, and call in the designated professionals if you have doubts about any injury.

Weather Hazards

Frostbite

Frostbite attacks the skin, often the cheeks, nose, and earlobes, and shows up as gray patches of skin. To help avoid frostbite, always ski or snowboard with a partner. Each partner should pay attention to the other's physical condition.

Hands and feet usually get cold first. Remember to wear warm gloves and socks. If your hands do get cold, swing your arms in circles to improve circulation and warm up your fingers. Use a heat pack if available. Try loosening your bootlaces, if your feet get cold, or try stamping your feet after unclamping your boots. When circulation returns and you are back on your skis or snowboard, try to move along rapidly to keep good circulation going.

To treat frostbite, take the following steps:

- Cover the frostbitten skin.
- Don't rub to improve circulation.
- *Never* rub frostbitten skin with snow; that makes the frostbite worse.

- Go inside the nearest shelter or ski lodge and get warmed up.
- Avoid too much heat from a fireplace, heater, heat lamp, or other concentrated source of heat.
- If the frostbite is severe, see a physician.

Hypothermia

Hypothermia occurs when the body loses more heat than it has produced, and the body temperature drops below normal. This is a serious, life-threatening condition.

Warning signs

- A cold day with temperatures in the 20°F to 30°F range (–7°C to –1°C).
- Shivering and fatigue.
- Pale skin, difficulty in speaking, person stumbles.

Treatment

- Add dry layers of clothes to get skier warmer.
- Give a warm drink. Hot chocolate is ideal.
- Get inside as soon as possible.
- To be safe, call a physician.

Avoidance

- Dress for the weather conditions, including the wind-chill factor.
- If a skier or snowboarder gets cold, stop and return to home base or find a shelter.
- Take regular water and snack breaks.
- Rest at least once every hour.
- Look out for others in your group; they, in turn, should look out for you.

- Make sure you have a partner. Arrange for partners to check on each other regularly.

- Keep checking for the first signs of frostbite or hypothermia.

Wind-chill factor

The wind-chill factor is a guide to how wind speed makes a body feel colder. For example, a temperature of 5°F and a wind speed of 10 mph will feel like a temperature of –15°F to your body. On cold and windy days, check both the temperature and the wind-chill factor and dress accordingly. Cross-country skiers know it is especially important to check wind speeds and any changes in the weather forecast.

Snow Blindness

Snow blindness is the loss of sight (usually temporary) caused by not wearing sunglasses or goggles to protect the eyes from ultraviolet rays reflected by snow or ice. Ordinarily, the eye's cornea and lens absorb UV rays, but when weather conditions are extreme, as can happen during skiing and snowboarding, this protection breaks down. The results are eye inflammation and a condition called *photophobia*, an inability to tolerate light. Snow blindness usually disappears after rest indoors, but the best insurance against this painful and frightening condition is to wear sunglasses or goggles.

Choose goggles or sport sunglasses with large tinted (gray, green, or yellow) shatterproof (polycarbonate) lenses to protect your eyes from the sun's ultraviolet rays. Snow and ice reflect 80–90 percent of the sun's rays, which are more intense at high altitudes. The National Weather Service issues a UV Index Forecast that indicates the amount of UV radiation expected in certain areas the following day. The index numbers range from 0 to 10+, with higher numbers indicating the largest amount of harmful UV radiation possible during the noon hour the next day.

Before snowboarding or skiing, check the UV Forecast and prepare yourself accordingly. If you wear glasses or contact lenses regularly, don't omit them on the slopes. Lenses can fog up, so use a spray or treated cloth to keep them clean. Carry extra saline or rewetting solution with you if you wear contact lenses, so your eyes don't dry out too much.

Sun and Wind Protection

Apply a sunscreen with a minimum Sun Protection Factor (SPF) rating of 15, even on cloudy days. Sunscreen is available with SPF ratings as high as 45 for children and those with very fair skin that burns readily.

Cold and wind at high elevations can cause chapped, dry lips, so carry a stick of lip balm to keep your lips moist and protected. Again, drink water whenever possible to help keep your entire body hydrated.

Minor Injuries

The following guidelines are suggested for treating minor injuries.

Scrapes and Burns

Wash scrapes and burns with an antiseptic cleaning solution and cover with sterile gauze. This is usually all that is needed to promote quick healing.

Blisters

Blisters can be problems for any athlete, and the best "medicine" is probably prevention. Properly fitting boots and socks can go a long way toward preventing this annoying, painful injury. Any blisters that do occur should be kept clean and covered with a bandage, especially if the blister breaks. Over-the-counter medications to treat blisters are available, but follow the suggestions of your instructor or doctor about using these.

Muscle Pulls, Sprains, and Bruises

Rest, ice, compression, and elevation (RICE) are the steps needed to handle these injuries and about all you should do in the way of treatment. Have the skier or boarder stop and rest, then apply ice, compress with an elastic bandage, and elevate the injured arm, leg, knee, or ankle.

Ice reduces swelling and pain and should be left on the injured area until it feels uncomfortable. Remove the ice pack and rest for 15 minutes, and then reapply. These are the immediate steps to take until a doctor arrives.

RICE reduces the swelling of most injuries and speeds recovery. Over the next few days, the injury should be treated with two to three 20-minute sessions per day at two and one-half hour intervals. This should provide noticeable improvement. Don't overdo the icing; 20 minutes is long enough. In most cases, after two or three days or when the swelling has stopped, heat can be applied in the form of warm-water soaks. Fifteen minutes of warm soaking, along with a gradual return to motion, will speed the healing process.

Seek the advice of a sports-medicine professional prior to starting your own treatment plan. Specially shaped pads are useful for knee and ankle injuries, and they can be used in combination with ice, compression, and elevation. For a simple bruise, apply an ice pack.

Head, Hand, and Foot Injuries

Normally, the eye can wash out most foreign particles by its ability to produce tears. If this doesn't work, use eye-cleaning solution to wash out the irritant. A few simple guidelines to follow are:

- If you get something in your eye, don't rub the eye or use anything dirty, such as a cloth or finger, to remove the irritant.

- With clean hands, pull the eyelid forward and down, as you look down at the floor.

- Flush with eyewash, or use a clean, sterile cloth, to remove any particle you can see floating on your eyeball.

If the foreign object remains, a clean gauze pad should be taped over the eye. A doctor should then examine the eye.

Jammed and/or broken fingers can be hard to distinguish, so use a cold pack to control swelling and pain. If there is no improvement within an hour, the injury should be X-rayed.

To safely move a person with an arm, wrist, hand, or leg injury, follow these steps:

- A finger with mild swelling can be gently taped to an adjacent finger.

- An elastic bandage may be gently wrapped around an injured wrist to give the wrist support. Do not wrap heavily, and do not pull the bandage tight.

- If the athlete has a possible broken leg or arm, the best approach is not to move the leg or arm in any manner. A cold pack can be used to lessen discomfort until medical personnel arrive, and the skier or snowboarder should be kept warm with a blanket or other covering to avoid shock.

Remember: Do not move a seriously injured skier or boarder, but get prompt medical attention or call for emergency aid. If you will have to wait for assistance, cover the person with a lightweight blanket, since warmth will reduce the chance of shock. A doctor should see a broken bone as soon as possible.

By following the guidelines in this chapter, the extent and severity of injuries can be reduced and treatment minimized, so that the skier or snowboarder can confidently return to the slopes.

11

Glossary

ACL Anterior cruciate ligament; part of the knee.

Aerials Acrobatic jumps performed in freestyle skiing and in the freestyle event at the Olympic Winter Games.

Alpine skiing Skiing downhill on a slope. Alpine events at the Olympic Winter Games include downhill, slalom, giant slalom, super giant slalom, and combined.

Alpine snowboards *See* Racing snowboards.

Backside The tail end of a snowboard, where the rider's heels rest; the side of the board to which one's back faces when riding.

Backside wall When standing at the top of the halfpipe, this is the left wall of the halfpipe for a rider in a regular snowboard stance, or the right wall for a rider in a goofy-footed stance.

Base The average snow depth, or foundation of packed snow, on a mountain. Also, the first coat of wax on skis.

Basket The webbed circle, or ring, near the end of a ski pole. The basket "plants" the pole in the snow and keeps it from sinking. The basket is used for pushing off and stopping.

Bevel The degree of angle to which the edges of a snowboard are tuned. Racing or carving snowboards should have a larger bevel than freestyle snowboards.

Biathlon An Olympic Winter Games sport that combines a cross-country skiing race with shooting at fixed targets along a course.

Bindings The combination of metal plates, buckles, and/or straps that grasp and hold boots to skis or snowboards. The bindings are set to release skis from boots during a fall.

Boat-cut skis Skis that are wider in the middle than at the tips and tails.

Camber The upward curve under the center of skis and snowboards.

Carving Using ski or snowboard edges to control speed and make turns on a hill or in between the gates of a run.

Catch air To jump or get yourself into the air, off the snow, usually after riding over a small hill or mogul. In moguls competitions, two "airs" are required in each run.

Catching an edge   This occurs when the edge of a ski or snowboard accidentally digs into the snow (sometimes catching an indentation made by another skier) and causes the skier or snowboarder to stumble or fall.

Christie turn   A skiing turn with the skis parallel.

Chute   The long ramp down from a ski tower or a steep trail surrounded by rocks. In the Nordic ski jumping event, a skier gains speed on the chute and soars off the end of the ramp.

Combined   An alpine event combining downhill and slalom.

Cross-country   *See* Nordic skiing.

Cornice   An overhang of snow, usually caused by wind.

Crevasse   A deep, hidden crack in a glacier.

Downhill   A synonym for alpine skiing. Also, an Olympic event in which the skier with the fastest time down the slope wins.

Downhill ski   The ski closest to the downhill part of the ski slope.

Edge   Metal edge of a ski or snowboard. Used for carving edges in the snow.

Fall line   The straightest (and steepest) line down any given ski or snowboard slope.

Fédération Internationale de Ski (FIS)   The internationally recognized governing body for skiing.

Free heel   *See* Nordic skiing.

Free riding   Snowboarding for fun or recreation on all types of terrain.

Free riding snowboard   All-purpose snowboard for freestyle, racing, or alpine snowboarding.

Freestyle   An Olympic skiing event that includes aerials and moguls. Freestyle snowboarding is primarily associated with tricks. Freestyle snowboarding events include halfpipe, quarterpipe, slope style, and snowboardcross (SBX).

Frontside   The front end of a snowboard, where the rider's toes rest; the side of the board to which the rider's chest faces when riding.

Frontside wall   When standing at the top of the halfpipe, this is the right wall of the halfpipe for a rider in a regular snowboard stance and the left wall of the halfpipe for a rider in a goofy stance.

Gaiters   Leggings that cover legs and ankles of a cross-country skier, worn to keep snow out of boots. The term "gaiter" is also used to describe a high, tubular collar worn to keep the neck warm.

Gates   Pairs of flexible poles used to mark the course in alpine and snowboarding giant slalom events. Skiers must ski between them.

Giant slalom (GS)   An alpine skiing event down a long course with a steep slope and gates, or a snowboarding event on a symmetrical course with gates.

Goofy stance Snowboarding stance where the right foot is on the forward portion (or nose) of the board. Also called the goofy-footed stance. The opposite of the regular-footed stance.

Halfpipe A snow chute or structure that is built for freestyle snowboarding, shaped like a cylinder, or pipe, cut in half with symmetrical walls of equal height and size. In the halfpipe event, snowboarders move down the fall line of the chute while performing tricks from wall to wall.

Hard boots Stiffer snowboard boots designed for racing or carving. These may be made of hard plastics to maximize support, as in alpine ski boots. Opposite of soft boots.

Heel edge The edge of the snowboard where the heels rest. Opposite of toe edge.

Heli skiing Off-trail skiing, which is reached by helicopter.

Herringbone step A step used by skiers to walk uphill with their skis in a V.

Huck A snowboard term, meaning to throw oneself off a jump into the air.

Kick The tip and toe rise of a snowboard.

Kicker A launching jump (ramp) from which aerial freestyle skiers catch air.

Kicking Pushing off from one ski and gliding on the other.

Klister A wax for skis that is used when the snow is slushy and melting.

Leash   A length of cord that attaches a snowboarder's front leg to the front binding to prevent the board from detaching and going down the slope without the boarder.

Light touring skis   Lightweight skis for use on prepared tracks. Good for beginning cross-country skiers.

Moguls   An event in freestyle skiing. Also, the snow-covered bumps or mounds on ungroomed slopes that are used in that event.

Mountaineering skis   Skis used by expert skiers in the wilderness. Mountaineering skis are lightweight, strong, and durable.

National Cross-Country Ski Education Foundation (NCCSEF)   Grassroots organization that promotes and helps to fund the sport of skiing.

Nordic skiing   Skiing across open country. Also known as cross-country, X-C, and free-heel skiing.

Nordic ski poles   Lightweight fiberglass poles with curved tips.

Nose   *See* Tip.

Off-track skiing   Skiing cross-country, but not in prepared tracks.

Parallel cut   Skis that are the same width from tip to tail. Used for track skiing and racing.

Plate binding   A snowboard binding system in which hard boots are attached by a flat metal plate to the board.

Poling Using ski poles to push off or to keep balanced when gliding, skating, or walking on skis.

Poma lift A surface lift with a platter-shaped disc for skiers to straddle and sit on as they're pulled up a hill.

Powder Freshly fallen or light, ungroomed snow.

Quarterpipe A halfpipe (snowboard course) with just one wall, normally used for attempting a single trick at a time.

Racing skis Parallel-cut skis that are the lightest weight and give the fastest response.

Racing snowboards The strongest snowboards, built for speed and steep slopes. Also called alpine snowboards.

Regular stance Standing on a snowboard with the left foot forward. Also called regular-footed stance. The opposite of the goofy stance.

RICE Acronym for Rest, Ice, Compression, and Elevation. The recommended treatment for muscle pulls, sprains, and bruises.

Rise The upward tilt of ski tips.

Runout The area at the bottom of a ski jump where the skier slows and stops.

Ruts The deepest section between the moguls on a hill.

Safety straps Straps attached from boots to ski bindings to keep the skis under control when the bindings are released.

Schussing Skiing downhill on a path along the fall line, often in a tuck position.

Shovel The upward curve of a snowboard. The curve at the front is called the tip shovel; the curve at the back is called the tail shovel.

Sidecut The narrow midsection (waist) of a ski.

Sidestep A step used by skiers to walk uphill sideways.

Skating skis Skis worn to make ice skating strokes in Nordic events and when skiing cross-country.

Slalom (SL) An alpine racing event involving gates. From the Norwegian words *sla* for slope, hill, or smooth surface, and *lom* for the track down the slope.

Slope-style snowboards Wide, fat, and soft boards for performing difficult maneuvers on the snow.

Snow blindness Serious condition that occurs when a skier or snowboarder does not wear sunglasses or goggles. Can cause permanent damage to the eyes if not treated immediately.

Snowplow A basic technique for slowing, turning, and stopping in which the front ski tips form a V (as if pigeon-toed). An easy way to control speed.

Soft boots Snowboard boots designed specifically for freestyle and free riding snowboarding. Soft and flexible, the boots offer a wide range of motion while still supporting the feet. Opposite of hard boots.

Stance In snowboarding, how the boarder positions the feet when standing on the board. *See also* Goofy stance; Regular stance.

Step-in binding A snowboard binding system, which can be used with soft or hard boots, in which the rider's boots snap directly into a binding attached to the board.

Stomp pad Nonskid pad between the bindings of a snowboard. Used to stand on when the back boot is not in the binding.

Super giant slalom (Super G) An alpine skiing event on a slope that is longer, wider, and has more gates than the giant slalom. Abbreviated as SG.

Superpipe A halfpipe course with larger, smoother transitions that allow snowboarders to get higher above the lip of the pipe.

Switchstance A snowboarding term for performing a trick while riding backward. The trick is performed exactly the same way it would be if the rider was riding forward. Also called a switch.

Tail The back of a ski or snowboard. The opposite of the tip (or nose).

Tail kick The underside curve of a snowboard at the back.

Takeoff The launch in freestyle (aerials) skiing off the end of the kicker. Good form on a takeoff includes arms, hips, and knees all completely extended as the skier's feet leave the end of the kicker.

Telemark turn A ski turn made while the skier is down on one knee with the skis parallel.

Tip The front (or nose) of a ski or snowboard.

Toe edge   The edge of a snowboard on which the toes rest. Opposite of heel edge.

Touring skis   Durable, heavy, and wide skis for the beginner.

Track skiing   Nordic skiing in prepared tracks.

Transition   The radial curved section of a halfpipe wall, between the vertical and flat bottom of a snowboarding course. A rider uses the transition to gain speed, catch air, and land. Also called the "tranny."

Traverse   To ride perpendicular to the fall line in skiing or snowboarding. In halfpipe riding, a snowboarder traverses from side to side or wall to wall.

Tucked position   Position used to gain maximum speed on a slope; the position always used by ski jumpers going down the chute.

Tuning   The process of checking equipment for proper condition before skiing or snowboarding.

Uphill ski   The ski nearest to the uphill part of the ski slope.

U.S. Ski and Snowboard Association (USSA)   The official national governing body for skiing and snowboarding in the United States, recognized by the United States Olympic Committee.

Vertical   In snowboarding, the top portion of the halfpipe wall that allows the snowboarder to fly out of the pipe, above the lip, and into the air. Also called the "vert."

Waist   The center section of a ski.

Wax   Hard or soft material applied to bottoms of skis to improve performance, speed, and maneuverability.

Wind-chill factor   A calculation based on the combination of wind speed and temperature, designed to indicate how cold the body actually feels.

X-C   *See* Nordic skiing.

Yard sale   A bad or wipeout fall in which a skier's skis, poles, hat, or other apparel are strewn on the ski slope or mountain.

12

Olympic, Skiing, and Snowboarding Organizations

The organization of, and participation in, the Olympic Games requires the cooperation of a number of independent organizations.

The International Olympic Committee (IOC)

The International Olympic Committee (IOC) was created by the Congress of Paris on June 23, 1894, and is entrusted with the control and development of the Modern Olympic Games, as well as sustaining the Olympic Movement worldwide. The Olympic Movement, an umbrella organization, consists of the IOC, the International Sports Federations, the 199 National Olympic Committees, the Organizing Committees for the Olympic Games, national sports associations, clubs, and the persons belonging to them, and, of course, the athletes. The Olympic Movement also includes other organizations and institutions that are recognized by the IOC.

Among the IOC's many responsibilities are determining the host city where the Games will be held, as well as approving the Olympic program of medal events for each Games. It is the obligation of the IOC membership to uphold the principles of the Olympic ideals and philosophy beyond any personal, religious, national, or political interest.

The members of the IOC are individuals who act as the IOC's representatives in their respective countries, not as delegates of their countries within the IOC. The members meet once a year at the IOC Session. They retire at the end of the calendar year of which they turn 70, unless they were elected before the opening of the 110th Session (Dec. 11, 1999). In that case, they must retire when they reach the age of 80. The term of office for all members is eight years, renewable every eight years. The IOC chooses and elects its members from among such persons as its nominations committee considers qualified. All Olympic Movement members have the right to submit nominations. There are currently 126 members (including 11 active athletes) and 22 honorary members.

The contact information for the International Olympic Committee and the IOC Museum and Olympic Studies Centre are:

IOC
Chateau de Vidy
Case Postale 356
1007 Lausanne, Switzerland
Tel: (+41 21) 621 61 11
Fax: (+41 21) 621 6216
Internet: http://www.olympic.org

IOC Museum and Olympic Studies Centre
Villa Olympique
1, Quai d'Ouchy
1006 Lausanne, Switzerland
Tel: (+41.21) 621.65.11
Fax: (+41.21) 621.65.12

The National Olympic Committees

National Olympic Committees have been created, with the design and objectives of the IOC, to prepare national teams to participate in the Olympic Games. Among the tasks of these committees is to promote the Olympic Movement and its principles at the national level.

The NOCs work closely with the IOC in all aspects related to the Games. They are also responsible for applying the rules concerning eligibility of athletes for the Games. Today there are 199 National Olympic Committees throughout the world.

The contact information for the U.S. Olympic Committee is:

United States Olympic Committee
One Olympic Plaza
Colorado Springs, CO 80909-5760
Tel: (719) 632-5551
Fax: (719) 578-4654
Internet: http://www.usolympicteam.com/

U.S. Ski and Snowboard Association

The United States Ski and Snowboard Association (USSA) is the national governing body for Olympic skiing and snowboarding in the United States and the representative to the United States Olympic Committee (USOC).

A nonprofit organization of volunteers that manages competitive skiing and snowboarding in the United States, the USSA offers development programs for younger and/or junior skiers and manages 14 men's and women's national teams who are preparing for competitions. The organization is responsible for helping U.S. skiers and snowboarders become successful at all levels of competition.

USSA trains the teams that represent the United States, and chooses, funds, and coaches these athletes and represents their interests as a member of the USOC. Also, the group administers memberships and technical services for its 30,000 athletes, coaches, officials, and volunteers. It is the licensing agency for skiers, snowboarders, coaches, and officials, and oversees all U.S. skiing and snowboarding competitions.

The organization offers licenses for different skiing levels:

- *Youth Competitor:* Age 12 and under in alpine skiing.
- *Student:* An alpine student who can participate in non-scored, non-advancement competitions.
- *Competitor:* Ranked on USSA's ranking list. Participates in some regional competitions and national events.
- *Masters:* Adult racers age 21 and over, who compete in various age categories. The Masters level leads to the U.S. Masters Championships.

The USSA also offers clinics for coaches and officials and collects dues for:

- Competitions
- The management of ranking lists
- The training of coaches and officials.
- Insurance for athletes and the USSA.

U.S. Ski Team Foundation

This Foundation raises the funds to support the USSA's eight ski and snowboard programs and 14 national teams. These funds come from membership dues, commercial sponsors, television, and licensing. Fund-raising events throughout the United States during the season are another source of support.

For event schedules, information on how to purchase merchandise, or other helpful links, visit the USSA web site or contact the USSA at:

U.S. Ski and Snowboard Association
P.O. Box 100 (1500 Kearns Blvd.)
Park City, Utah 84060-0100
Tel: (435) 649-9090
Fax: (435) 435-3613
Internet: http://www.usskiteam.com
           http://www.ussnowboard.com

Other Skiing and Snowboarding Associations

International Ski Federation/Fédération Internationale de Ski (FIS)
Blochstrasse 2
CH-3653 Oberhofen
Switzerland
Tel: (+41 33) 244 6161
Fax: (+41 33) 243 5353
Internet: http://www.fis-ski.com/

International Snowboard Federation (ISF)
Pradlerstr 21
A-6020 Innsbruck
Austria
Tel: (+43) 512 3428 34
Fax: (+43) 512 3428 34 2

U.S. National Ski Hall of Fame and Museum
Box 191
Ishpeming, MI 49849
Tel: (906) 485-6323
Fax: (906) 486-4570
Internet: http://www.skihall.com/

International Ski History Association (ISHA)
499 Town Hill Road
New Hartford, CT 06057
Tel: (860) 738-7788
Fax: (860) 738-7788

Cross Country Ski Areas Association
259 Bolton Road
Winchester, NH 03470
Tel: (603) 239-4341
Fax: (603) 239-6387
Internet: http://www.xcski.org/

National Ski Areas Association
133 South Van Gordon Street, #300
Lakewood, CO 80228
Tel: (303) 981-1111
Fax: (303) 986-2345
Internet: http://www.nsaa.org/

Professional Ski Instructors of America
133 South Van Gordon Street, #101
Lakewood, CO 80228
Tel: (303) 987-9390
Fax: (303) 988-3005

SnowSports Industries America
8377B Greensboro Drive
McLean, VA 22102
Tel: (703) 556-9020
Fax: (703) 821-8276
Internet: http://www.snowlink.com/

Organizing Committees

Salt Lake Organizing Committee (SLOC)
299 S. Main St., Suite 1300
Salt Lake City, UT 84111-2241
Tel: (801) 212-2002
Fax: (801) 364-7644
Internet: http://www.saltlake2002.com
(XIXth Olympic Winter Games dates: Feb. 8-24, 2002)
(VIIIth Paralympic Winter Games dates: March 7-16, 2002)

Turin Olympic Organizing Committee
Turin Organizing Committee for the XXth Olympic Winter Games
Via Nizza 262/58
10126 Torino, Italy
Tel: (+39) 011 631 0511
Fax: (+39) 011 631 0500
Internet: http://www.torino2006.it
(XXth Olympic Winter Games dates: Feb. 11-26, 2006)

Sports Organizations for Athletes with Disabilities

United States Association of Blind Athletes
33 North Institute St.
Colorado Springs, CO 80903
Tel: (719) 630-0422
Fax: (719) 630-0616
Internet: http://www.usaba.org/

United States Cerebral Palsy Athletic Association
25 West Independence Way
Kingston, RI 02881
Tel: (401) 792-7130
Fax: (401) 792-7132
Internet: http://www.uscpaa.org/main.htm

USA Deaf Sports Federation
3607 Washington Blvd., Suite 4
Ogden, UT 84403-1737
TTY: (801) 393-7916
Fax: (801) 393-2263
Internet: http://www.usadsf.org/

Disabled Sports USA
451 Hungerford Drive, Suite 100
Rockville, MD 20850
Tel: (301) 217-0960
Fax: (301) 217-0968
Internet: http://www.dsusa.org/

Dwarf Athletic Association of America
418 Willow Way
Lewisville, TX 75067
Tel: (972) 317-8299
Fax: (972) 966-0184
Internet: http://www.daaa.org/

Special Olympics International
1325 G Street, NW, Suite 500
Washington, DC 20005
Tel: (202) 628-3630
Fax: (202) 824-0200
Internet: http://www.specialolympics.org/

Wheelchair Sports, USA
3595 East Fountain Blvd., Suite L-1
Colorado Springs, CO 80910
Tel: (719) 574-1150
Fax: (719) 574-9840
Internet: http://www.wsusa.org/